DATE DUE			

DISTRICT
MEDIA
SERVICES

APS

ALBUQUERQUE PUBLIC SCHOOLS

WORLD BOOK'S
YOUNG SCIENTIST

WORLD BOOK'S

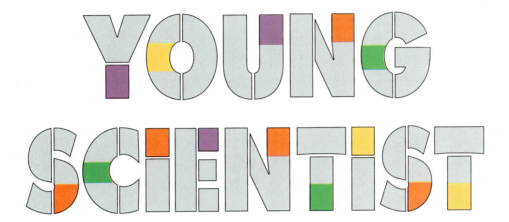

YOUNG SCIENTIST

Volume 6

World Book, Inc.
a Scott Fetzer company
Chicago   London   Sydney   Toronto

Activities that have this warning symbol require some adult supervision!

The quest to explore the known world and to describe its creation and subsequent development is nearly as old as mankind. In the Western world, the best-known creation story comes from the book of Genesis. It tells how God created the earth and all living things. Modern religious thinkers interpret the Biblical story of creation in various ways. Some believe that creation occurred exactly as Genesis describes it. Others think that God's method of creation is revealed through scientific investigation. *Young Scientist* presents an exciting picture of what scientists have learned about life and the universe.

Contents

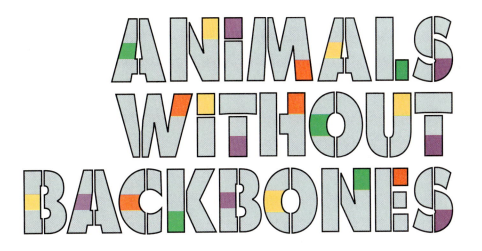

These are invertebrates

An **invertebrate** is an animal that doesn't have a backbone. Of all the millions of animals in the world, only about 40,000 different kinds, or **species,** have backbones. By far the greater group is the invertebrates. Scientists have already given names to more than one million species of invertebrates.

Invertebrate animals include **sponges; corals** and **jellyfish; worms; starfish** and **sea urchins; mollusks** such as snails and octopuses; and **arthropods** such as insects, spiders, and crabs.

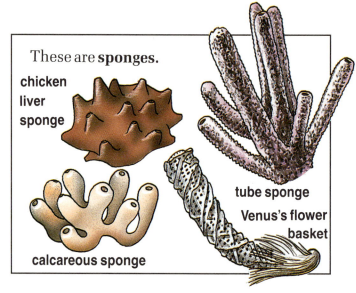

These are **sponges.**

chicken liver sponge

calcareous sponge

tube sponge

Venus's flower basket

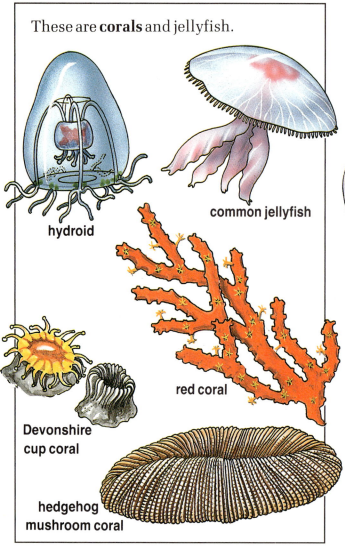

These are **corals** and jellyfish.

hydroid

common jellyfish

red coral

Devonshire cup coral

hedgehog mushroom coral

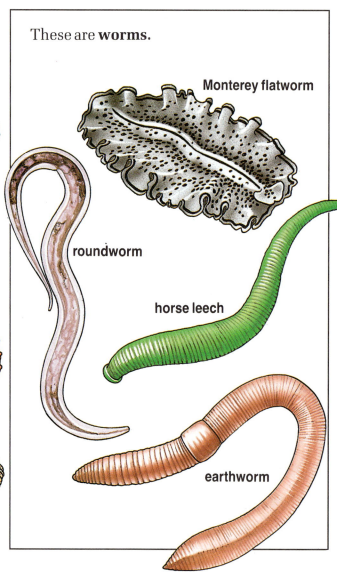

These are **worms.**

Monterey flatworm

roundworm

horse leech

earthworm

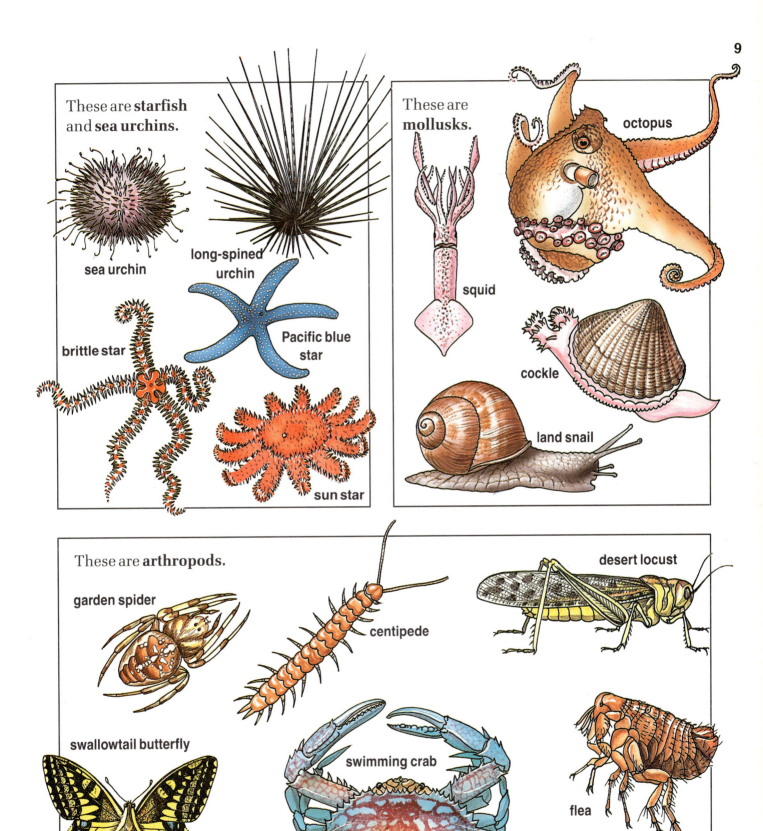

These are **starfish** and **sea urchins**.

sea urchin

long-spined urchin

brittle star

Pacific blue star

sun star

These are **mollusks**.

octopus

squid

cockle

land snail

These are **arthropods**.

garden spider

centipede

desert locust

swallowtail butterfly

swimming crab

flea

This bright red sponge has attached itself to the rocks and is growing across the rock surface.

What is a sponge?

If you see a sponge, you will probably think it is a plant, not an animal. **Sponges** are underwater invertebrates with no heads, arms, legs or internal organs. Adults don't move about from place to place. They attach themselves to rocks or plants and stay in one place all their life. It's no wonder that even scientists once thought sponges were plants!

What made scientists decide that sponges were animals? Scientists discovered that sponges get the food they need in the same way as other animals do—by eating other living creatures. This is an important difference between animals and plants. Plants can make their own food and do not need to eat other living creatures.

Find out more by looking at pages **50–51**

There are about 5,000 different species of sponge. This number doesn't include the sort of sponge that's made in factories for us to wash and clean with! Sponges grow in many different shapes and sizes. Some species of sponge are tiny and are no bigger than a large coin, but others grow to be more than 40 inches (1 meter) wide.

Most sponges live in the salty water of warm oceans. A few live in fresh water, such as lakes and rivers. If you see a sponge that is bright yellow or orange or brown, it is sure to come from salt water. If it's a green sponge, it will come from fresh water. But purple or gray sponges can live in either salty water or fresh water.

Inside a sponge

Even though they may be shaped differently, all sponges work in the same way. A sponge takes in water through small **pores,** or holes, called **ostia.** The water contains oxygen and lots of tiny plants and animals for the sponge to eat.

After the sponge has absorbed the oxygen and food that it needs to live, it pushes the water out through one large pore called an **osculum.** The water takes with it waste products the sponge no longer needs.

water out

osculum

ostia

water in

What are jellyfish and corals?

Have you ever seen a jellyfish? It looks like an umbrella with projections, called **tentacles,** hanging down from the edges. The body of a jellyfish is like a hollow bag with thick sides. These sides have an "outer skin" and an "inner skin." Between these two "skins" is a jelly-like substance. This substance gives the jellyfish its shape. Jellyfish live in the sea, but they are not fish. Fish have backbones and move forward by swimming. Jellyfish do not have backbones, and they move up and down in a unique way. They expand like an opening umbrella, then pull together again rapidly. This squeezes water out from beneath, and the jellyfish moves upward.

Jellyfish eat small sea animals after stinging them with their tentacles. The tentacles are covered with thorny threads. When another animal bumps into the jellyfish, these threads lash out like tiny, poisonous whips. The threads paralyze the victim, and the jellyfish then uses its tentacles to pull the trapped animal into its mouth.

Danger!

If you see a jellyfish, even one that has been washed up on the beach, don't touch it. The poison from some jellyfish stings can be deadly to human beings. Anyone stung by a sea wasp, a kind of Australian jellyfish, will almost certainly die within a few minutes. Common jellyfish sting but do not kill.

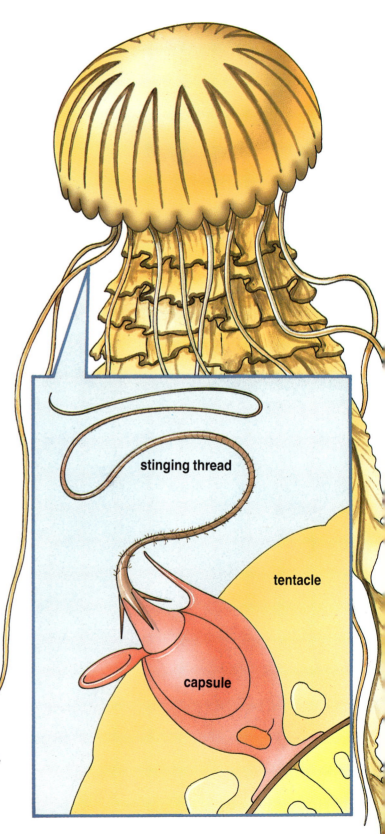

stinging thread

tentacle

capsule

The tentacles of a jellyfish are covered with tiny capsules. Inside each capsule is a thorny, stinging thread. The jellyfish whips out these threads to paralyze small animals.

Find out more by looking at
pages **50–51**
56–57

13

The polyps of this coral have a mouth surrounded by tiny tentacles. These catch food floating past in the water.

Coral animals

Corals live in the sea, too, but they stay in one place all their life. Corals that stretch over large areas are called **reefs** and can be very colorful. Each reef is made up of millions of individual coral animals, called **polyps.** Polyps may live singly or together in large groups called **colonies.**

Each tiny polyp has a body shaped like a hollow cylinder, or tube. This is attached at one end to the seabed, the reef, or even another polyp. At the other end, the polyp's mouth is surrounded by tiny tentacles. Polyps eat tiny plants and animals that they filter from the seawater with their tentacles.

Why are jellyfish and corals alike?

Jellyfish and corals belong to a group of invertebrates called **coelenterates.** The term **coelenterate** means "hollow body." Why are these two very different animals in the same group?

Ribbon worms are long, flat worms that are often brightly colored. Most live in the sea, but a few kinds of ribbon worm live on land or in fresh water.

What is a worm?

All worms have soft, thin bodies with no legs. There are thousands of different kinds, or species, of worm. Some worms are so small that you need a microscope to see them. Others grow as long as 10 feet (3 meters).

Roundworms

Biologists sort worms into four very different groups. The biggest group is that of roundworms. Roundworms, such as hookworms and vinegar eels, have bodies like pieces of thread. Most roundworms are very small—scientists once counted 90,000 in one rotting apple! Some roundworms live in water, some live on land, and others live inside animals, plants, or humans. Animals which live in or on other living things are called **parasites.** Hookworms are parasites that can live in your body and will make you ill.

Ribbon worms

Most ribbon worms live in the sea. They are long and flat, like ribbons. Ribbon worms eat other small animals, including worms and mollusks. A ribbon worm, such as the bootlace worm, catches its food by shooting out a long tube called a **proboscis** from the top of its head.

Segmented worms

The bodies of segmented worms, such as the earthworm and the leech, are divided into sections, called **segments.** These make the worm look as though it has rings around its body. Most leeches live in water. Leeches have a flat body with a sucker at each end. They use the front sucker to feed on the blood of fish and other animals that live in the water.

Flatworms

Another group of worms is called flatworms. Some flatworms look like oval-shaped leaves, and others look like long ribbons. Many species of flatworm live in the sea, but some flatworms, called planarians, live among the stones and tiny plants found in freshwater lakes and streams. Flukes and tapeworms are flatworms that are parasites. These flatworms commonly live inside the bodies of humans, where they can cause serious illnesses.

Adult flukes live commonly in the bloodstream of people who inhabit parts of Africa and the Far East. These flukes cause a serious disease called bilharzia (or schistosomiasis).

 15

Find out more by looking at
pages **16 – 17**
　　　　 32 – 33

The life cycle of a fluke

1. The eggs of the fluke pass into the water through human waste.

2. In the water the eggs hatch into young creatures, called **larvae,** that swim about.

3. The young larvae enter the bodies of water snails where they change into a different shape.

4. The larvae leave the water snail and burrow into the skin of animals and humans swimming around them.

5. Once the larvae get into the bloodstream of humans and animals, they grow into adult flukes.

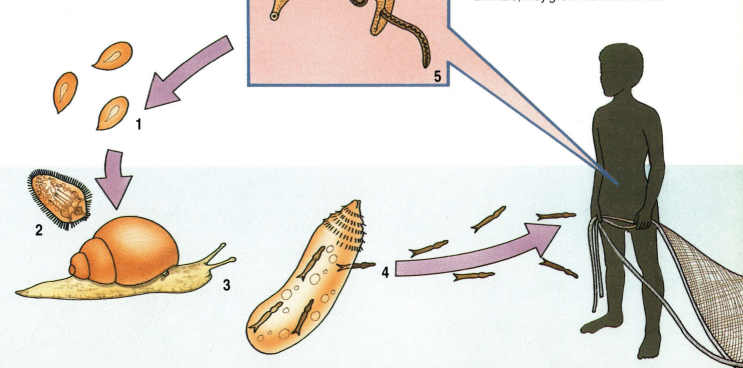

Earthworms live in moist, warm soil in many parts of the world. The small, orange-colored band in the center of the worm's body shows that it is an adult. Earthworms have segmented bodies.

Watching earthworms

Earthworms usually live just below the surface of the soil. As they tunnel through the earth, these segmented worms take in soil and small pieces of dead plants. The plants are the earthworm's food. The soil passes through the earthworm's body and is pushed out at the other end in little corkscrew-shaped piles, called **worm castings.**

An earthworm moves by stretching out its body in front and then pulling in its back end. Along its body are tiny hairs, called **bristles,** that stop the earthworm from slipping. If you rub your finger underneath a large earthworm, you can feel these bristles.

Earthworms are useful creatures. Their tunnels allow air to reach the roots of plants, and this helps the plants to grow. Earthworms eat leaves and other dead plant material in their tunnels. The waste matter that they leave behind then rots or **decays.** This decayed material adds nutrients to the soil. **Nutrients** improve the condition of the soil for plants to grow.

You will need:

powdered chalk

various types of soil, such as sand, earth or peat

two plastic bottles, one large and one small

Making your own wormery

You can see for yourself how earthworms tunnel through the soil by putting them into a special container called a **wormery.** Watch the worms stretching and pulling in their bodies as they move through the tunnels.

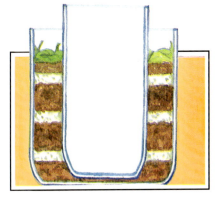

1. Ask an adult to help you cut the tops off both bottles. Place the small bottle inside the larger one, and put a layer of one kind of soil around the outside of the small bottle.

2. Sprinkle some powdered chalk on top of the first layer. The chalk will help you to see the worm tunnels more easily.

3. Fill up the large bottle in this way, with another layer of a different kind of soil and then another layer of chalk. Leave a space of about 1 inch (2.5 centimeters) at the top.

4. Add a layer of dead leaves or grass cuttings at the top and sprinkle enough water to moisten the soil, being careful not to saturate it.

5. Now dig up a few large earthworms from the ground and put them in the space at the top of your wormery.

6. Cover your wormery with a cloth, because worms don't like the light. Leave it for a day before looking to see what the worms are doing. Always keep your wormery covered when you are not looking at it, and don't forget to water it lightly when the soil feels dry.

What are starfish and sea urchins?

Starfish, sea urchins, sea cucumbers and sand dollars belong to the same group of invertebrates that live in the sea. All these animals are **echinoderms,** which means ''spiny skinned''. Their bodies look different, but they are all round in some way. Sea urchins are shaped like a ball. Starfish are flatter and have disk-shaped bodies, with a number of arms around the outside of the central body.

Starfish

Have you ever found a dead or stranded starfish on the beach? Most starfish have five arms, but some species have as many as fifty! If you turn a starfish over, you'll see hundreds of tiny, sucker-like tubes waving about on the undersides of its arms. These are **tube feet,** and they are very useful to the starfish. The suckers on the tube feet can stick to rocks or shells. The starfish moves along by pushing out, or extending, the tube feet on one of its arms so that they will stick to a nearby rock or to the seabed. When the tube feet shrink, or contract, the starfish is pulled forwards.

Each tube foot has little strength, but hundreds of tube feet together are much stronger. Starfish use their tube feet to pull apart the shells of clams and oysters so that they can eat the soft flesh inside. To eat, the starfish pushes its stomach out of its mouth and folds it around the food! Starfish are not fish and do not have gills to take in oxygen from the seawater. Instead, they use their tube feet to absorb oxygen from the water.

This common European starfish has lost one of its five arms, but a new arm is already growing. Starfish are able to grow new arms to replace ones that have been lost.

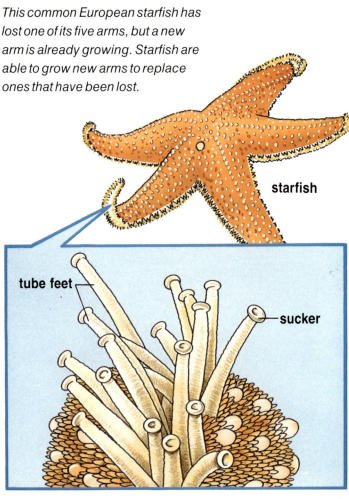

starfish

tube feet

sucker

The undersides of the arms of the starfish are covered with hundreds of tiny tubes called tube feet.

Sea urchins

Have you ever found a shell on the beach that's shaped like a ball with small holes in it? This sort of thin, fragile shell, called a **test,** is probably the shell of a dead sea urchin. The holes in the test show where the sea urchin's tube feet once stuck out. Most sea urchins use their tube feet to crawl along the seabed, but some move along using the long spines that cover their body.

Sea urchins have sharp teeth to chew their food. They are **scavengers,** which means that they feed on decaying matter. But they also eat seaweed and small animals living on rocks or on the seabed.

Find out more by looking at pages **48 — 49**
52 — 53

The hard shell, or test, of each of these sea urchins is covered in long spines and tiny tube feet with suckers. Some sea urchins use these tube feet to crawl and also to collect food.

Find out more by looking at
pages **48–49**
       52–53
       54–55

What is a mollusk?

A **mollusk** is an invertebrate animal with a soft body and no bones. Mollusks include snails, mussels, and oysters. Each of these has a hard shell on the outside that protects its soft body. Some mollusks, such as cuttlefish and squid, have hard shells that grow inside their bodies. Octopuses and slugs are also mollusks. Octopuses have no shell at all.

Some mollusks live in water, and others live on the land. All mollusks need to keep their bodies moist to stay alive. So those that live on the land find their way to damp places. They bury themselves in sand or soil, or crawl under leaves.

The soft body of the octopus makes it different from most kinds of mollusks. Using its eight arms, the octopus can crawl on the seabed and move through the water to catch its food.

Snails

Many snails that live in fresh water eat plants and dead animals. Ocean snails feed on seaweed and other sea creatures. Land snails often eat rotting plants. Although most snails are small, some grow to be 2 feet (61 centimeters) long. Many snails are an important food for fish and birds. But some snails are poisonous, and others carry certain diseases.

Bivalves

Mussels, oysters, and clams belong to a group of mollusks called **bivalves.** Bivalves have a hard outer shell made up of two halves that are held together by a hinge. Bivalves live in water, and most of them live in the sea. Bivalves usually have their shells open so they can feed on tiny pieces of food from the water that they pump through their bodies. When a bivalve is frightened, or taken out of the water, it closes its shell tightly.

Octopuses

Octopuses have eight long arms, called tentacles, whose undersides are covered with suckers. They eat crabs, shrimps, and other small creatures caught with their tentacles.

A snail of most species has a soft body covered with a tube-like shell. This shell coils around itself as it grows. A snail's shell starts growing before the snail hatches, and stops growing only when the snail becomes an adult.

Clams are mollusks that live on the bottoms of oceans, lakes, and streams in many parts of the world. Two popular food clams are the hard-shell clam, *above,* and the soft-shell clam, *below.*

What is an arthropod?

Do you know what a beetle, a butterfly, a crab and a spider have in common? All these invertebrate animals have legs with more than one section. The parts that join these sections together are called **joints.** The animals' bodies are also made up of separate sections or segments, with a stiff outer covering called an **exoskeleton.**

Beetles, butterflies, crabs, and spiders belong to a large group of invertebrate animals called **arthropods.** More than three-quarters of all the different species of animals living on our planet are arthropods. Biologists are still finding hundreds of new species of arthropods every year.

Centipedes and millipedes are arthropods. Their bodies are divided into many segments. Each segment has one or two pairs of legs. Some millipedes have 115 pairs of legs!

Spiders and scorpions are a kind of arthropod called an **arachnid.** All arachnids have eight legs.

Insects, such as cockroaches, beetles, bees, and butterflies, are also arthropods. All insects have six legs.

Another group of arthropods, called **crustaceans,** includes crabs, lobsters, wood lice, water fleas, and shrimps. Crustaceans have several pairs of legs.

Some crab spiders hide in flowers to catch flies and bees. They can change color from white to yellow to match surrounding flowers.

A centipede can have as many as 170 pairs of legs. Each pair of legs is attached to a segment of the centipede's body.

Find out more by looking at
pages **28 – 29**
38 – 39
52 – 53

Fiddler crabs can be found beneath the sand or mud in tropical or temperate regions. Each male fiddler crab has a large claw to attract female crabs and to fight with other males.

The damsel fly rests its two pairs of wings on its back when it is not flying. Its large eyes help it to find food when flying above the water's surface.

A naturalist's diary

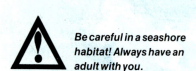

Be careful in a seashore habitat! Always have an adult with you.

A person who is interested in watching and learning about living things is called a **naturalist.** Are you a naturalist?

How can you learn about invertebrate animals? One good way is to look for places where invertebrates live and to watch them in their natural surroundings. We call an animal's immediate natural surroundings its **habitat.** You would have to swim under the sea to watch corals, jellyfish, or octopuses in their natural habitat! But you can find other sea creatures, such as crabs, shrimps, and clams, in tide pools or under the sand near the seashore at low tide.

Many invertebrates that live on the land need to keep their bodies moist. Where would you look to find them? Good places to look are under stones and logs, and among dead leaves. Be sure to replace anything you move, so that the animals can carry on with their lives as before you came.

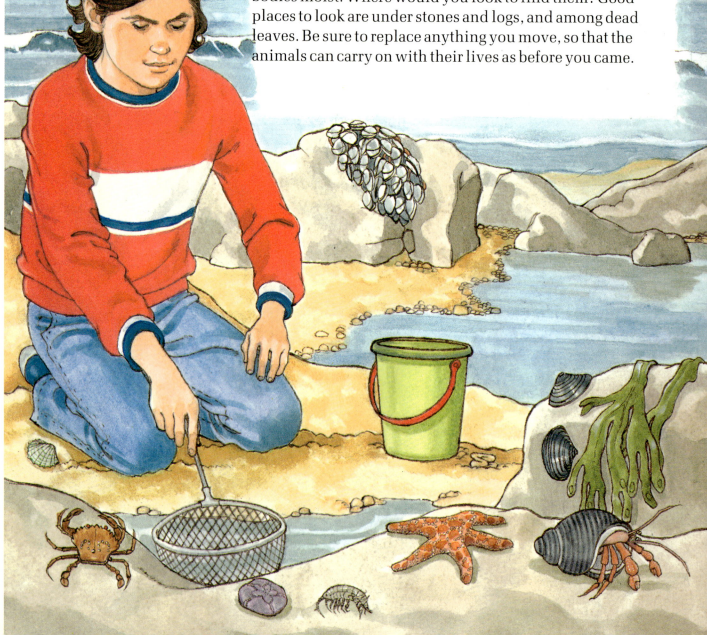

Keeping a record

You will need:

a pencil

a notebook

1. All good naturalists keep a record, or diary, of the living things that they find. The words and pictures you record in your notebook will remind you what you found, and where and when you found it.

2. Write down the date and the time of day. Describe the habitat and the weather. Next, write down as much as possible about the creatures that you can see. What are the creatures called? How many are there? How do they move? What are they doing? What are they eating?

3. If you find a creature and you don't know its name, you can draw it in your notebook and find its name in a reference book later on. Your notebook will become your own reference book.

Make sure that you record the shape and color of the creature. You can show the right size of the creature by drawing a straight line the same length as the creature next to your drawing.

4. If you have a camera, you can take photographs of the creatures in their habitat to put in your notebook later.

It is difficult to find some invertebrates because they match their surroundings so well. This bush cricket is almost the same color as the leaf beneath it.

Watching invertebrates

There is always a reason for everything that an animal does. When you are watching invertebrates, can you guess why they behave as they do?

Daily behavior

Most of an animal's daily behavior has something to do with one of three basic needs. Every animal needs food, oxygen, and shelter.

An animal can stay alive only if it has food to eat and oxygen to breathe. Animals also need some kind of shelter to protect them from bad weather, or from enemies that might kill and eat them.

Butterflies do not usually fly when their wings are wet. This brimstone butterfly is finding shelter under a leaf during a rain shower.

You will need:

some dry soil

some newspaper

a sheet of plywood

a sheet of thin, clear plastic

a watering can

about 20 wood lice

a plastic tray or shallow box

What do wood lice like?

Wood lice are harmless invertebrates that live on land. They need to make sure that their bodies don't dry up. So they live in dark, damp places, like in tree bark or under stones or leaf litter. You can see this for yourself by doing a simple experiment. Be sure to handle the wood lice carefully.

1. Put some soil in the tray and press it down firmly. Cover one half of the tray with newspaper, and water only the open half. Then remove the newspaper.

2. Put the tray in a dimly lit place and put the same number of wood lice in each half of the tray. The wood lice in the dry half will move about quickly.

3. Cover the tray with the board. Wait for 20 minutes and then lift the board and count the wood lice in each half of the tray. What have you found out?

4. Add more water to the tray so that both sides are moist. Cover the tray with the plastic sheet and darken one side with the newspaper. Wait several minutes and take a look. What have the wood lice done?

When you have finished your experiment, don't forget to put the wood lice back where you found them.

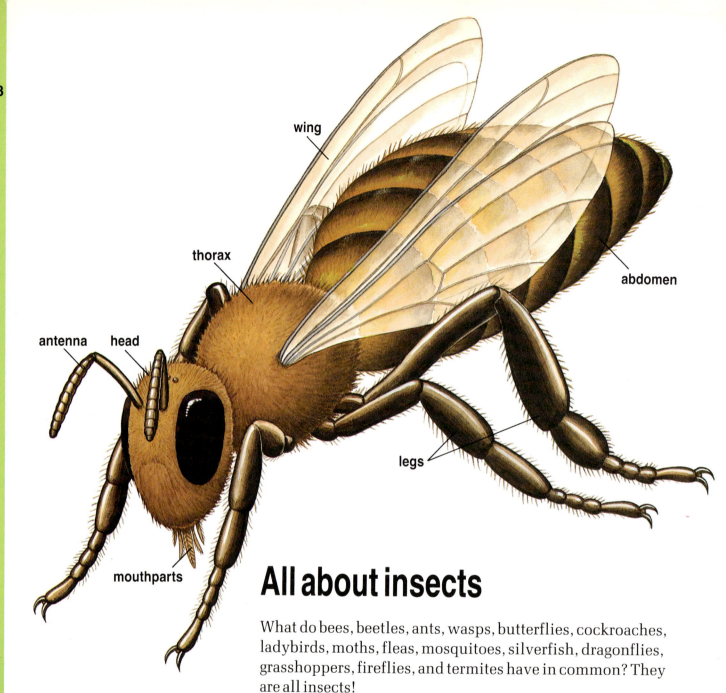

wing

thorax

antenna   head

abdomen

legs

mouthparts

Insects are a kind of arthropod. Like all insects, the honeybee has a body made up of the head, the thorax, and the abdomen. It also has three pairs of jointed legs.

All about insects

What do bees, beetles, ants, wasps, butterflies, cockroaches, ladybirds, moths, fleas, mosquitoes, silverfish, dragonflies, grasshoppers, fireflies, and termites have in common? They are all insects!

Do you know how many different kinds of insects there are? Scientists have given names to one million different kinds of animals, and more than three-quarters of these are species of insects. Yet every year, biologists discover between 7,000 and 10,000 new insect species which they hadn't recorded before. Some scientists believe that there may be as many as 10 million different kinds of insects on our planet.

An insect's body

The body of an insect is made up of three different sections— the head, the thorax, and the abdomen.

The springtail is a tiny, wingless insect that can jump long distances. Springtails usually live in damp places.

On its **head,** an insect has eyes, mouthparts, and feelers called **antennae.** The insect's mouth is an opening in its head, with mouthparts nearby that either chew or suck food. Grasshoppers chew plants. Many beetles and cockroaches chew both plants and small creatures. Bedbugs and horseflies suck blood from animals and humans. Butterflies usually suck a sweet liquid, called nectar, from plants.

The middle section of an insect's body is called the **thorax.** The insect's legs and wings are all attached to the thorax. Insects are the only invertebrate animals that have wings. Most adult insects have wings, but not all insects can fly. Insects can be classified into smaller groups according to the number of their wings. Houseflies, tsetse flies, and mosquitoes have two wings. Moths, butterflies, bees, and wasps have four wings. Dragonflies have four wings and can fly as fast as 60 miles (97 kilometers) an hour.

The **abdomen** of an insect contains the working parts, or organs, that digest the insect's food and get rid of waste products. The organs needed for reproduction are also inside the abdomen.

Drawing insects

You will need:

a pencil

a notebook

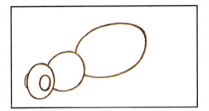

1. An insect's body has three parts, so start by drawing three simple shapes to show the head, the thorax, and the abdomen. Add small circles for the eyes.

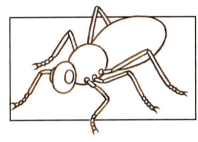

2. An insect has six legs which are attached to the thorax in three pairs. When you draw the legs, remember that the back legs are longer than the front ones.

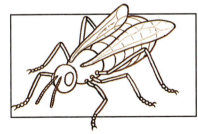

3. Most insects have antennae on their head and wings on their thorax. If the insect you are drawing has antennae and wings, draw them in now.

Insects that live together

Some insects live together, forming a large community where every individual has a part to play. These **social insects** include ants, termites, wasps, and honeybees.

Termites

There are about 2,000 different species of termites. Most termite species live in warm countries. Millions of these ant-like insects can live and work together in a huge nest, or **colony.** Worker termites build the nests. Some species build huge, strange-looking mounds with bits of soil mixed with saliva. Inside the nest, a complicated network of tunnels allows fresh air to flow through the colony and to control the temperature.

There are four different types of termites. Each type has a body suited to the work it does. A single queen termite lives with her king in a special chamber deep inside each nest, where she is well protected. The queen termite is bigger than all the others. Although she has legs, she is too heavy to move about. Small worker termites bring her food to eat, and she lays thousands of eggs. Some tropical queen termites can lay as many as 30,000 eggs a day. The worker termites then take the eggs away to nursery chambers, where the eggs are looked after by specialized nurse workers. Other worker termites look after the chambers in the nest.

The nest is protected by soldier termites, which have huge jaws, hard heads, and strong legs. They defend the colony against enemies, usually ants. The soldier termites are also wingless and blind. Unable to care for themselves, they must be fed by the workers.

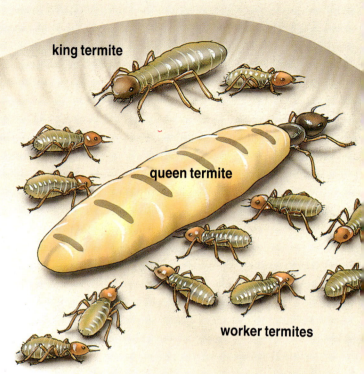

king termite

queen termite

worker termites

Thousands of termites live in this strangely shaped mound of mud. Termite nests can sometimes reach a height of 20 feet (6 meters).

soldier termites

Honeybees

Thousands of honeybees live together in a colony called a **hive.** In any hive there are three different types of honeybee. The largest is the **queen bee.** Each hive has only one queen bee. She lays all the eggs in the colony, sometimes as many as 2,000 in one day.

Male honeybees are called **drones.** They have only one function, and that is to mate with the queen. After mating, the queen can lay eggs for the rest of her life.

All the other honeybees are female. They are called **worker bees** because they do all the work but they do not mate. Some worker bees, called **foragers,** go out of the hive to collect food. Honeybees feed on the powder called pollen and the sugary liquid called nectar, both of which they find in flowers. Forager bees pass the nectar to other worker bees, and the worker bees store it in open cells. Meanwhile, some worker bees look after the young honeybees, and others guard the hive. Every honeybee has its own job to do.

Honeybees collect pollen from flowers and store it in tiny pollen 'baskets' on their back legs. They then take it back to the hive.

larva

pupa

adult

citrus swallowtail butterfly

The caterpillar passes through several stages before becoming a butterfly. The adult butterfly develops inside the chrysalis, or pupa.

Insect life cycles

Scientists use the term **life cycle** to describe the different stages in the life of an animal. During their life cycles, most invertebrates produce new young animals like themselves. This process is called **reproduction.** Most invertebrates need a male and a female of the same species to reproduce.

Moths and butterflies

Most insects lay eggs. The eggs of moths, butterflies, flies, beetles, ants, and wasps hatch into young called **larvae.** Caterpillars are the larvae of butterflies and moths. Insects, such as butterflies, pass through several stages from being an egg to becoming an adult. This amazing change is called **metamorphosis.**

The larva changes into a sort of legless shell called a **chrysalis,** or **pupa.** The body of the adult insect forms inside the pupa and comes out fully grown later.

You will need:

a sheet of strong paper

string

a few caterpillars

a handful of moss

a few twigs

a pencil

a supply of fresh green leaves

some potting compost

a large clear jar

a tray

a notebook

Watching a metamorphosis

1. Put the potting compost in the bottom of the jar with the moss and twigs.

2. Find some caterpillars on a plant outside. Collect two or three on a tray with some green leaves taken from the plants you found them on— they won't eat just any leaves.

Grasshoppers and locusts

The eggs of grasshoppers, locusts, termites, and cockroaches hatch into **nymphs.** These look just like the parent insects except that they have undeveloped wings and sex organs. The nymphs change their skin several times as they grow bigger, and their wings and sex organs gradually develop.

Springtails and bristletails

Springtails and bristletails do not go through a stage of being larvae or nymphs at all. Instead, the eggs hatch into miniature copies of their parents.

Life cycle kits

In the United States, most biological supply houses advertise life cycle kits. Butterfly kits are also popular. Perhaps an adult can help you find such a kit.

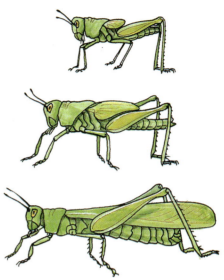

A young grasshopper looks like the adult grasshopper, but it has no wings. The wings develop when the insect is fully grown.

3. Put the caterpillars into the jar. Make a lid for the jar with the paper and string.

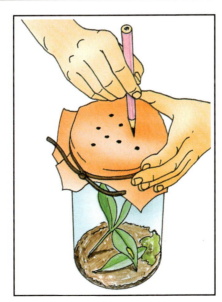

4. Pierce a few holes in the paper lid with the point of the pencil.

5. Give your caterpillars fresh food from the right kind of plant each day. Keep a record of what you see each day. When the pupae become butterflies or moths, let them go free.

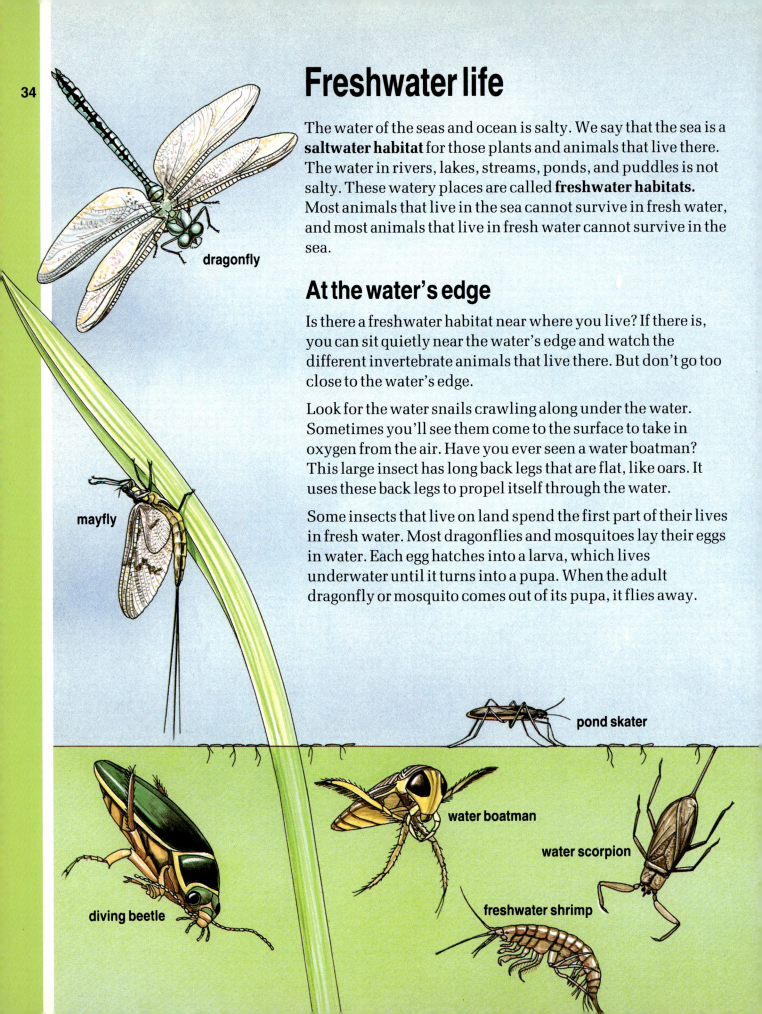

Freshwater life

The water of the seas and ocean is salty. We say that the sea is a **saltwater habitat** for those plants and animals that live there. The water in rivers, lakes, streams, ponds, and puddles is not salty. These watery places are called **freshwater habitats.** Most animals that live in the sea cannot survive in fresh water, and most animals that live in fresh water cannot survive in the sea.

At the water's edge

Is there a freshwater habitat near where you live? If there is, you can sit quietly near the water's edge and watch the different invertebrate animals that live there. But don't go too close to the water's edge.

Look for the water snails crawling along under the water. Sometimes you'll see them come to the surface to take in oxygen from the air. Have you ever seen a water boatman? This large insect has long back legs that are flat, like oars. It uses these back legs to propel itself through the water.

Some insects that live on land spend the first part of their lives in fresh water. Most dragonflies and mosquitoes lay their eggs in water. Each egg hatches into a larva, which lives underwater until it turns into a pupa. When the adult dragonfly or mosquito comes out of its pupa, it flies away.

dragonfly

mayfly

pond skater

water boatman

water scorpion

diving beetle

freshwater shrimp

Collecting plankton

Plankton are tiny plants and invertebrate animals that drift near the surface of both seawater and fresh water.

Working around water requires adult supervision and help!

You will need:

20 inches (50 centimeters) of strong wire

a strong stick, about 40 inches (1 meter) long

strong nylon cord

an old nylon stocking

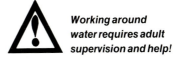

a small glass jar

scissors

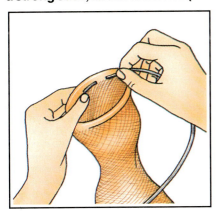

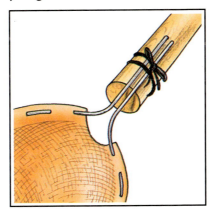

1. Thread the wire in and out through the top of the stocking, bending it into a circle about 8 inches (20 centimeters) across.

2. Join together the two ends of the wire. Use the cord to fasten the wire firmly to the stick.

3. Cut off the foot of the stocking. Use the cord to tie the bottom of the stocking tightly around the neck of the jar.

4. Pull the net through either seawater or fresh water to collect plankton in the jar.

Making an observation cell

To look closely at the plankton, it's a good idea to make a small container called an **observation cell.**

You will need:

two pieces of stiff, clear plastic, about 4 in × 4 in (10 cm × 10 cm)

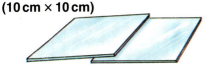

a magnifying glass

modeling clay

1. Join the two pieces of plastic together with modeling clay along three edges. Leave a space of about ¼ inch (6 millimeters) between the pieces. This is your observation cell.

2. Fill the space between the plastic with water from your plankton jar, and examine the plankton with a magnifying glass.

Collecting land invertebrates

Pick up a handful of forest or garden soil. Can you see anything moving around in it? In that handful of soil there are hundreds of living things. Most of them are tiny **bacteria** and **fungi**—living things that are too small to see without a microscope. Can you see some small invertebrate animals crawling about in the soil? These invertebrates feed on the bacteria and fungi, and then larger animals feed on them!

Adult supervision and help are needed for parts of this activity.

You will need:

fresh soil

a small bucket

white paper

a notebook and pencil

a fine strainer

a magnifying glass

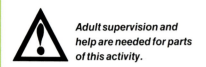

a plastic bottle

a glass jar

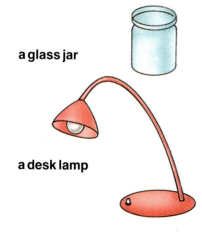

a desk lamp

Looking at soil animals

1. Collect some fresh soil in the bucket. You'll find many different kinds of invertebrates if you take the soil from among the dead leaves underneath a tree.

2. Place a few handfuls of soil into the strainer and shake it onto the white paper. Use the magnifying glass to see if any animals have fallen through onto the paper.

3. Now make a funnel to collect small creatures from the soil. Ask an adult to help you cut the bottom off a plastic bottle. Place the top part of the bottle upside down over a jar.

4. Put some dead leaves and soil into the bottle, and hold it under a lamp. The animals will move away from the heat and light of the lamp and fall into the jar.

Draw the animals you have seen in your notebook, and try to find out what they are from a reference book.

Making an ant farm

You will need:

a small, narrow glass jar

a larger, wide-mouth jar with lid

can opener

cheesecloth

moist sand

ants

string or rubber band

1. Put a 1-inch (2.5 cm) layer of moist sand in the larger glass jar.

2. Find an ant hill in a dry place where the soil is loose. Poke the hill with one of the sticks and catch a few ants that come out.

3. Place the ants into the small glass jar. Put this jar upside down on the sand inside the larger jar and put the cover on the larger jar.

4. Fill the space between the two jars with the moist sand.

Poking the holes requires adult supervision and help.

5. Poke holes in the jar lid with the can opener. Cover the top with cheesecloth, fastened with the string or rubber band.

6. Watch the ants burrow through the sand for a few days. Their network of passageways will amaze you.

Life cycles on the land

All spiders start life as an egg. The mother spider spins a bag of silk around her eggs to protect them. The bag is known as an **egg sac.** The eggs of most species of spider are left to hatch on their own. The babies of some species of spider are attached to thin threads of silk that carry them away on the wind. They land in different places so that not all the new, hungry baby spiders are looking for food in the same place.

A female wolf spider carries a bag of eggs with her. Even after they have hatched, the young wolf spiders live on their mother's back for a few days until they are big enough to look after themselves.

female spider with egg sac

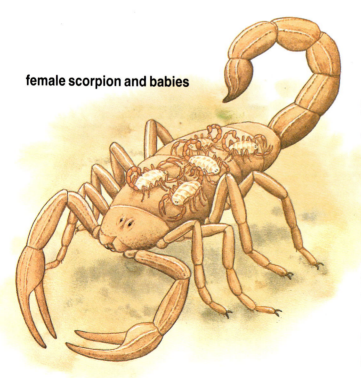
female scorpion and babies

Scorpions

When scorpions mate, the male faces the female and holds on to her pincers. They may both lift their tails in the air. They then move backward and forward. The male produces sex cells, called **sperm,** that enter the female's body to fertilize her eggs. Scorpions do not lay eggs. Instead, baby scorpions develop internally from eggs in their mother's body. When the babies are born, they are small copies of their parents. The babies live on their mother's back for a few days before they set out to hunt for themselves.

Crustaceans

Most crustaceans live in water. Early in life they are larvae that look very different from their parents. Wood lice are one of the few groups of crustaceans that live on land. Wood lice eggs hatch into tiny copies of the adult animals.

Find out more by looking at
pages **16–17**
20–21
22–23

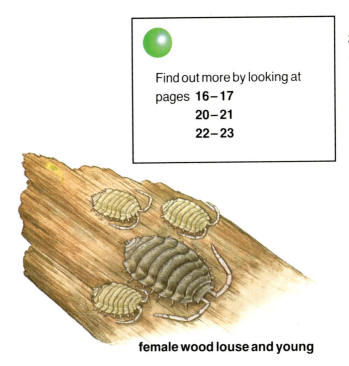

female wood louse and young

land snails and eggs

Snails

Land snails hatch from eggs. There are no distinct males or females. Snails are **hermaphrodites,** which means that each snail has both male and female sex organs in its body. Land snails lay their eggs in clusters in holes in the ground. The eggs of large land snails have hard shells. Each newly hatched snail is a small copy of its parent.

Earthworms

Earthworms are hermaphrodites, too, but adult worms mate so that they can reproduce. When earthworms join together to exchange sperm, fertilized eggs are produced in a sort of belt around their bodies. As the earthworm moves along, this belt slides off its body and closes completely around the eggs to form a package called a **cocoon.** The cocoon protects the eggs until they are ready to hatch into tiny new earthworms several weeks later.

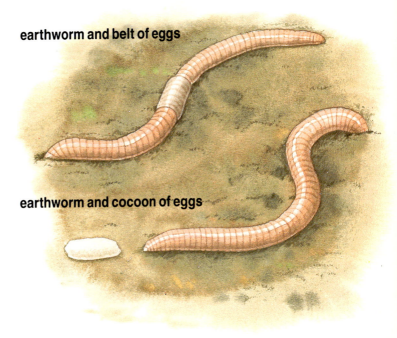

earthworm and belt of eggs

earthworm and cocoon of eggs

Find out more by looking at pages **24—25**

Among the grasses

As you walk through long grass on a fine day you will often see all sorts of creatures moving out of your way. Butterflies flutter away, grasshoppers jump from stem to stem, spiders and beetles run under leaves or roots. Thousands of species of invertebrates live in **grasslands.** Some live only where the grass is short, and others live only in long grass.

If you want to know more about these grassland invertebrates, you could watch them through a magnifying glass. You could draw them in your notebook and look them up later in a reference book. Or you could catch several species in a special net called a **sweep net,** or in small **pitfall traps. Remember** that some of these animals sting or bite, and others have sharp bristles that can prick you. Be careful when you handle these animals, and let them go when you have finished looking at them.

You can catch invertebrates living in long grass by using a sweep net. Nets come in a variety of sizes and shapes. The mesh should allow air to sweep through. Find out in the library how to make your own net.

Setting pitfall traps

Find out more about grassland invertebrates by catching them in a pitfall trap.

You will need:

a garden trowel or an old spoon

some small pieces of hardboard

some plastic cups

1. Dig some holes in the ground that are just big enough for the cups to fit into.

2. Put two cups, one inside the other, in each hole. Make sure that the rim of the top cup is level with the top of the soil when you push them all the way down.

3. Put a piece of hardboard over each trap to keep out the rain. Prop up this cover on some small stones so that there is a gap of about ¾ inch (2 centimeters) between the top of the cup and the hardboard. Don't use glass as a cover, because it will make the trap too hot when the sun shines.

Look inside your traps regularly. Take out the inner cup to examine your catch closely. Then let the animals go and put the cup back in position.

Put your traps in different parts of the grassland. Is it possible to catch different kinds of animals in short and long grass? Are the animals that fall into your traps at night the same kinds as you catch during the day? Try putting small bits of fruit or meat or sugar water into the traps. Does this make any difference in the number of animals that you catch? Remember to fill in the holes when you've finished your activity.

These bark beetles are tunneling through the bark of an elm tree. This type of beetle spreads a disease, called Dutch elm disease, that kills the elm trees. This disease is a major environmental problem in North America.

Invertebrates in the woodlands

Do you have a large group of trees near you? In some countries, this would be called woodlands, or woods, or simply bush. Woodlands are home for thousands of species of invertebrates, and many of these animals eat leaves.

Which invertebrates live in trees?

You don't have to climb up a tree to find out which invertebrates live in it. Just spread a large sheet of paper or cloth on the ground below the tree, and hit the branch above the sheet with a strong stick. Hit it hard, just once. Now look at the animals that have fallen onto the sheet. You might find caterpillars, beetles, and a few spiders. Most of these creatures can find their own way back into the tree, but you'll have to help the caterpillars back onto the leaves.

Lower down on the tree, you may find insect larvae living just under the bark. Where some pieces of bark have fallen off, you might see the marks of tunnels where beetle larvae have been living. These tunnels are called **galleries.** Among the ferns and flowers of the woodland, look for holes in the leaves, where caterpillars and other invertebrates have been eating them.

Each year the leaves of some trees die and fall onto the woodland floor. Invertebrates such as springtails and mites live among and feed on the fallen leaves.

The marks on this tree trunk are tunnels made by bark beetle larvae.

Apples that aren't fruits

Oak trees grow in several parts of the world. If you look on the small branches or twigs of an oak tree in the hot season, you will see lots of small, brown, spongy balls called **oak apples,** or **galls.** Galls are not real fruits, but are made when the larvae of insects feed on the tree. If you open up a gall, you can see larvae inside. Larvae can also be seen inside banyan tree fruits and figs.

Galls can damage fruit trees and food crops, such as wheat. If you find a gall with no holes in it, you'll know that the larvae are still inside. Put the gall into a glass jar with a piece of cloth over the top, and wait to see the gall insects coming out.

Tropical rain forests

Thick green woodlands grow in some parts of the world. Here, it's always hot, and rain falls nearly every day. These woodlands are called **tropical rain forests.** They are home to hundreds of different kinds of vertebrate animals and thousands of different plants and invertebrates. A larger variety of species lives in a rain forest than in any other kind of habitat. Scientists studying the rain forests in Indonesia have discovered more than 2,500 species of insects living in just five different kinds of trees!

Invertebrates in the trees

Thousands of insects can live on one tree in a tropical rain forest. About one-quarter of these insects, mostly caterpillars and adult beetles, will eat the tree's own leaves, or the leaves of the climbing plants that grow on the tree.

Tiny insects called aphids feed on juice, or sap, which they suck from the stems or leaves. The aphids then produce a sweet liquid called **honeydew.** This honeydew attracts some ants that nest in the tree and others that just visit to collect it from the aphids. Bees and flies feed on the pollen in the tree's flowers. Some flies are so small that they can tunnel through the insides of the leaves, eating them as they pass through.

Velvet worms live on the moist floor of tropical rain forests. They eat worms and insects.

Some flying insects, such as mosquitoes, live in water during the larval stage of their life cycle. In a rain forest, pools of water will collect where branches join the trunk of the tree. Or water might be trapped between the leaves of climbing plants. Mosquitoes breed here. They live together with the tadpoles of tree frogs.

Many wasps, beetles, and crickets eat plants and small animals. Lacewings, tiger beetles, and assassin bugs hunt other insects, such as aphids.

Some rain forest insects lay their eggs either inside, or on top of, other invertebrates. This sort of insect is a parasite. The other living thing that the parasite lives inside or on is called a **host.** Many rain forest insects are scavengers, which eat dead leaves or the left-over food of other animals. Some, such as dung beetles, feed on droppings of other animals.

Many ants make their homes underground, but these tropical ants in Sierra Leone have built their nest in a tree.

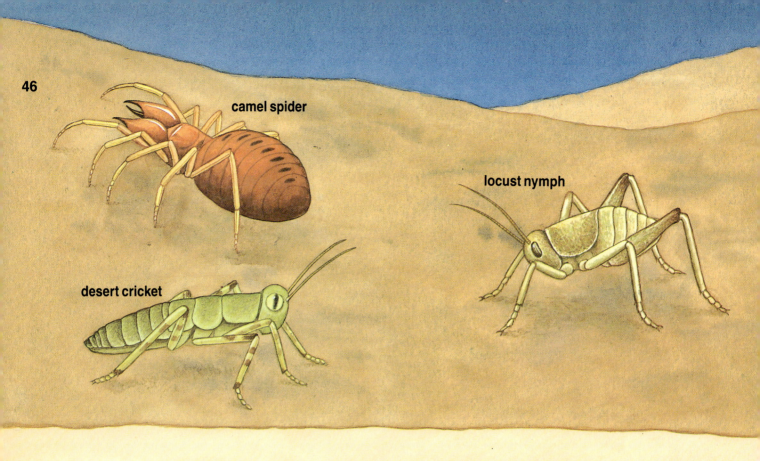

camel spider

locust nymph

desert cricket

darkling beetle

Darkling beetles

Some darkling beetles walk in the desert during the day. These beetles have long legs that keep their body raised off the hot ground. Certain darkling beetles always stand with some of their feet lifted off the ground. They change from one set of feet to another every few seconds.

In the desert

Many large areas of land in the world are **deserts.** There are several kinds of desert, but every desert is very hot during the day, very cold at night and very dry for much of the year. As a rule, less than 10 inches (25 centimeters) of rain falls in a desert in a year. Some deserts may receive no rain at all for many years. Animals that live in the desert need to avoid the heat and to live on very little water for a long time.

Staying in the shade

Most desert animals come out of their hiding places only in the cool of the evening. They avoid the heat of the day by hiding in holes under rocks or in burrows below the ground.

Desert scorpions come out to hunt only at night. They eat insects, spiders and lizards.

Camel spiders, also known as wind scorpions, are desert hunters with enormous jaws. They are not really spiders or scorpions, but are related to both. They come out at night to catch all sorts of small animals, including lizards and scorpions.

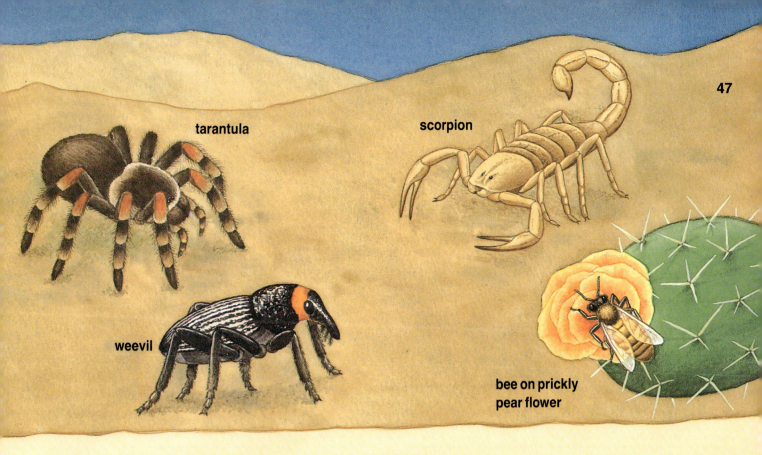

tarantula

scorpion

weevil

bee on prickly
pear flower

Surviving in the desert

Most desert invertebrates will drink water wherever and
whenever they find it. When there is no water, invertebrates
get the moisture they need from eating plants. Many desert
insects and spiders have watertight skins that not only keep
water out, but also help to keep moisture in their bodies.

Some desert invertebrates leave their shelter only after it has
rained. The rain makes the desert plants and flowers bloom.
Butterflies and bees emerge from their pupae and feed on
these flowers. Then these insects breed quickly. Before the
desert dries up again, the pupae of the next generation of
butterflies and bees are already developing. These pupae
emerge as adults when the next rains arrive.

Some shrimps stay as eggs for a long time when it's hot and
dry in the desert. When it rains, young shrimps quickly hatch
and complete their life cycle by growing into adult shrimps.
The adults lay more eggs before the desert dries up again, and
then they die.

Invertebrates in the sea

Nearly three-quarters of the earth's surface is covered by seas and oceans. Millions of different plants and animals live in the salt water of these seas and oceans.

Scientists divide all the living things in the sea into three groups, according to which layer of the sea they live in. The plants and animals that live near the surface of the water are called **plankton.** Those that live deep down on the seabed are called **benthos.** The animals that swim between the top and bottom layers are called **nekton.**

Tiny plants and animals

The plankton species that live in the sea are different from those that live in fresh water. Most of the plankton in the sea, including many kinds of algae, are plants called **phytoplankton.** Animal plankton are called **zooplankton.** Many zooplankton are so small you need a microscope to see them. Other zooplankton that live in the sea are the larvae of larger animals, such as crabs, barnacles, or squid. Jellyfish are the largest kind of zooplankton in the sea. Some jellyfish are nearly 80 inches (2 meters) wide.

Beneath the surface of the sea

Most of the nekton that swim about in the sea are vertebrate animals, such as fish, turtles, and sea lions. The nekton also include some invertebrates that can swim, such as squid and octopuses.

Most of the animals that live on the bottom of the sea are invertebrates. Some of the benthos animals stay in one place all their lives. Corals, sponges, and oysters attach themselves to the seabed or to rocks or reefs. They feed by filtering tiny plants and animals from the water. Starfish, worms, sea snails, crabs, and lobsters also live at the bottom of the sea. These animals walk or crawl from one place to another looking for food.

Plankton

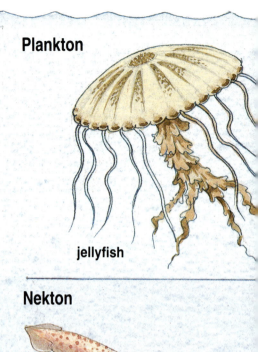

jellyfish

Nekton

Benthos

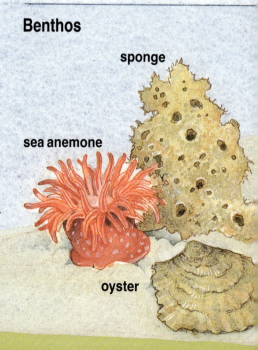

sponge

sea anemone

oyster

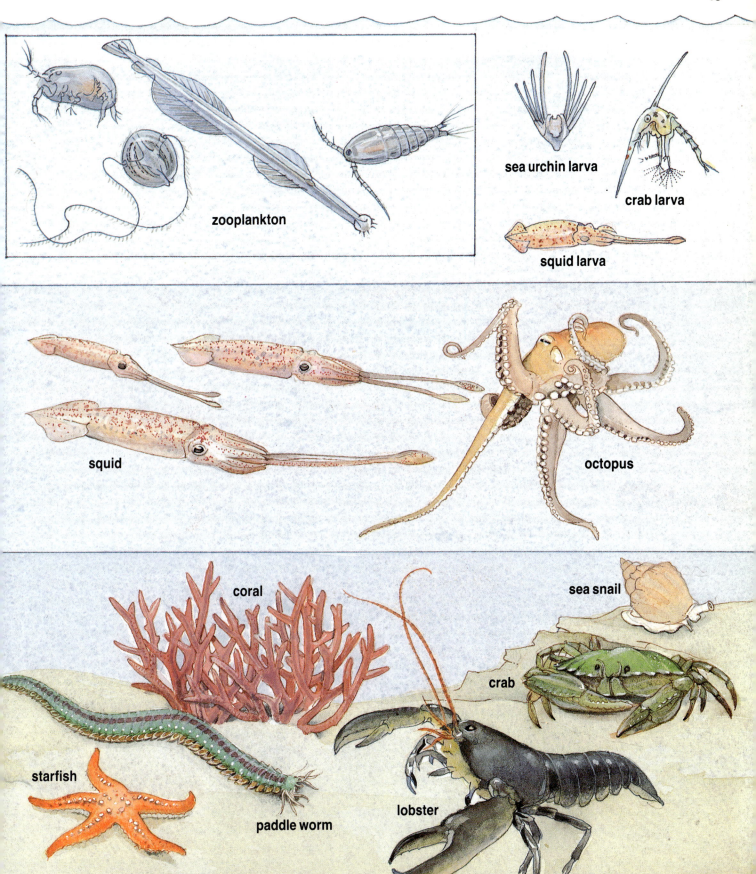

zooplankton

sea urchin larva

crab larva

squid larva

squid

octopus

coral

sea snail

crab

starfish

paddle worm

lobster

Life cycles in the sea

Many of the invertebrate species that live in the sea go through life cycles. Let's look at the life cycles of two groups of invertebrates — sponges and jellyfish — and see how they develop from eggs into adults.

Sponges

Some species of sponge start life as an egg, while others begin as small knobs called **buds.** The egg is a female sex cell that starts to grow inside the body of the parent sponge. Before it can grow into another sponge, the egg must be fertilized by a male sex cell, or sperm. Some species of sponge can produce both the egg and the sperm. These species can fertilize their own eggs.

Other species produce only eggs or only sperm. The male of the species releases sperm into the water. Then the sperm enter the female through the holes, or pores, in her body and fertilize the eggs.

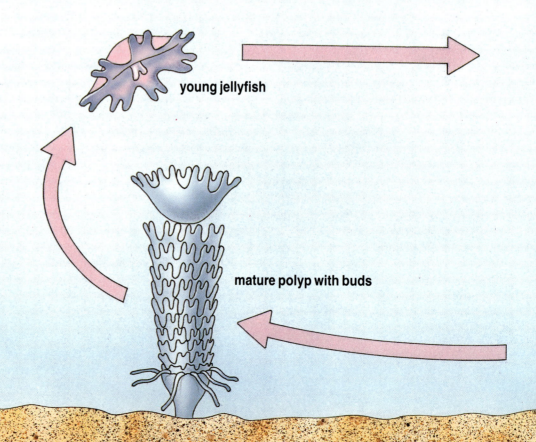

young jellyfish

mature polyp with buds

Where do new sponges come from?

Each fertilized egg grows into a round larva covered with tiny hairs called **flagella.** The larva uses the flagella to swim out of the parent sponge's body and into the water. After a few hours, or even days, the larva attaches itself to the sea-bed and grows into a new sponge.

In some species, the small knob-like buds from the parent sponge grow into new sponges. Sometimes they grow while still attached to the parent, and sometimes they break away and grow separately.

Jellyfish

Some species of jellyfish produce their young from eggs. The eggs grow into hollow cylinders, called **polyps,** which attach themselves to the seabed. New jellyfish start to grow on these polyps. Each bud of a mature polyp looks like a tiny saucer. When a bud is big enough, the polyp releases it into the sea and it grows into an adult jellyfish.

In the jellyfish life cycle, eggs are produced. These grow into tiny polyps. When the polyps are mature, they release buds that become adult jellyfish.

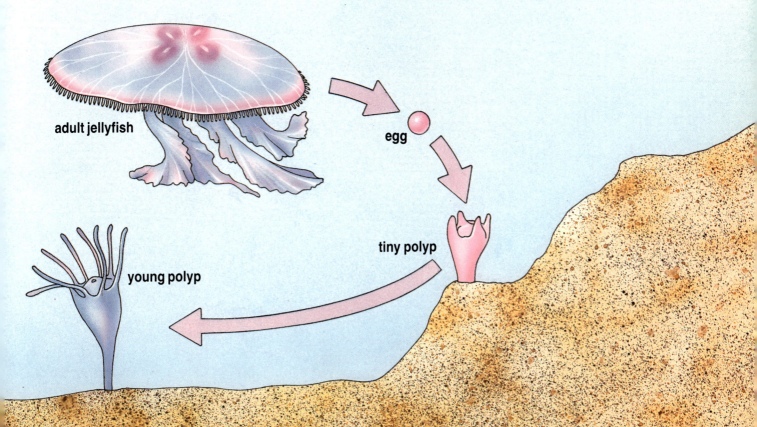

adult jellyfish

egg

tiny polyp

young polyp

Young creatures in the sea

Crabs, lobsters, and shrimps are all crustaceans that live in the sea and begin life as tiny eggs.

As the female lays her eggs, they are fertilized by sperm that the male has put on her shell. The female carries the fertilized eggs on her body until they hatch. When the eggs first hatch, the young—whether they are crabs, shrimps, or lobsters—don't look like their parents at all. They are small, legless larvae.

As they grow, the larvae change their skin and also their shape. The outer skin, or exoskeleton, of a crustacean is hard and can't get any bigger. So when the animal grows in size, it has to break out of its existing exoskeleton and grow a new, bigger one. This process is called **molting.**

As baby crabs molt, they grow bigger. The larvae of shrimps and lobsters molt and become more and more like the bodies of their parents. All crustaceans molt several times, even after they have become adults.

The female crab carries the eggs on certain parts of her body until they hatch into tiny larvae. Each larva changes its shape and size several times before becoming an adult crab.

female crab with eggs

newly hatched crab larva

adult crab

Find out more by looking at
pages **18 – 19**
20 – 21
22 – 23

Starfish and sea urchins

The eggs of starfish, sea urchins, and their relatives hatch into larvae. These larvae swim about before settling on the seabed. When they grow into adults, they lose their ability to swim!

Octopuses

Octopus eggs are almost transparent. A female octopus looks after her eggs for about two months until they hatch. That's quite a job, because she lays as many as 180,000 eggs at a time! In the two months between the times the eggs are laid and hatching, the female doesn't eat at all. When the young octopuses hatch out, they are like tiny copies of their parents. Each baby octopus is less than ½ inch (13 millimeters) long.

The female octopus lays long strings of eggs under the rocks. She guards the eggs carefully and cleans them with her tentacles.

On the seashore

Wherever the sea meets the land, there's an area called the **seashore.** The seashore may be flat or a high, steep cliff. The seashore becomes covered by deep water at high tide. At low tide, you can explore parts of the seashore. But be careful. And remember that not every shore has two tides a day.

Have you ever explored the seashore, looking for small animals? They cling to rocks, burrow under the sand, and live in the pools of water that collect among the rocks.

On the rocks

The small, round shells that look like little tents clinging to the rocks are limpets. Limpets have a soft, flesh-like "foot" that sticks fast to the rock when the tide is out. When the tide comes in, limpets crawl over the rocks, feeding on seaweed. The bluish-black shells on the rocks are mussels. Mussels cling to the rocks with strong, silky threads that they spin themselves.

Limpets live in this tide pool among the algae and seaweed.

Lugworms suck in the mud or sand, digest any food in it and push the waste up to the surface. Little piles of mud or sand, known as castings, tell you where the worms are.

Creatures under the sea

Some seashore animals bury themselves in the wet sand when the tide goes out. Birds know where to look for these animals. Watch where the birds are digging with their long bills, and you might be able to dig up some clams or other bivalves to look at. Don't forget that you're heavier than a bird. You might not be able to tread on very soft sand or mud without sinking in! Use a stick to prod the sand before you walk on it. And don't keep the clams away from the cool, damp sand for too long, or they will dry up and die.

Tide pools are the most interesting places on the seashore. Look for prawns moving quickly across the bottom of the pool. Can you see a starfish hiding under the seaweed? Snails crawl over the seaweed, while crabs wait with their claws open hoping to catch anything that passes by. If you tie a small piece of meat on a string and hold it near a crab, the crab might grab it so tightly that you can pull it out of the water and take a closer look. Be careful!

Make a rockpool viewer

You will need:

scissors

a small sheet of clear polyethylene

nylon string

a small plastic bucket

Ask an adult to help you cut the bottom out of an old plastic bucket. Place the polyethylene across the bottom and up the sides. Tie the string around the bucket to hold the polyethylene in place. You'll be surprised how much easier it is to see things with this viewer. Be sure an adult is with you at the tide pool.

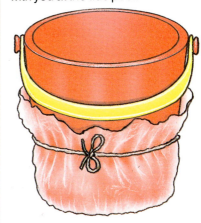

Coral reefs are found in warm, tropical seas. This colorful coral is growing in the Red Sea, which lies between Africa and Saudi Arabia.

Gardens in the sea

Look at the branches of a tree waving in the air. Some coral animals under the sea look just like miniature trees. They wave gently in the water. Corals grow in hundreds of different shapes and sizes. Many corals look like leafy plants, such as lettuce, or like mushrooms. Corals grow together in huge colonies that spread out like beautiful underwater gardens.

Each coral shape is made up of the remains of lots of small animals called polyps. A polyp has a soft body that's protected by a small, hard "skeleton." This is made of limestone and shaped like a cup. The "skeletons" of lots of polyps join to make a coral.

When a polyp dies, it leaves its "skeleton" behind, and new young polyps grow on top of it. This is how coral reefs and coral islands are formed. Living coral grows in many different colors, but the remains of dead polyps are usually white. Most of a coral reef is made up of limestone from the bodies of dead polyps.

The biggest coral reef in the world is in the sea of the northeast coast of Australia. Called the Great Barrier Reef, it is about 1,250 miles (2,010 kilometers) long. Yet the Great Barrier Reef has been formed by polyps that range in diameter from less than 1 inch (2.5 centimeters) to 1 foot (30 centimeters).

Life in a coral reef

Coral reefs and coral islands grow only in warm, clear, shallow waters. If you were lucky enough to swim by a coral reef, you would see thousands of colorful fish, crabs and other animals moving through the underwater garden. Clams and sponges attach themselves to the coral. Octopuses and eels hide in caves that form in the reef. Sea cucumbers help to keep the reef clean by eating small animals and plants, such as algae, that grow in between the corals.

Some of the animals that live among the coral are harmful to the reef. Some worms and mollusks tunnel into the limestone and weaken it. Some fish and starfish feed on the living coral. If all the living coral is eaten away, the sea quickly destroys the rock that's left behind. Parts of the Great Barrier Reef are in danger because thousands of crown-of-thorns starfish are eating away large areas of the living coral there.

Find out more by looking at pages **12–13**

The crown-of-thorns starfish lives in tropical waters. One of its favorite kinds of food is the reef-building coral.

Find out more by looking at pages **30–31**
32–33

What is a pest?

A pest is a nuisance! A **pest** is a plant or an animal that causes harm to another living thing. Termites, woodworms, and death-watch beetles eat wood and damage homes. The larvae of some moths feed on clothes and curtains. Some species of mosquito suck human blood and spread the tiny parasites that cause a dangerous disease called malaria.

Insect pests

Locusts and weevils are insects that are pests to farmers. Locusts eat the crops while they are still growing, and weevils eat food, like grain, that has been harvested and stored. Some farmers spray their crops with chemicals that are poisonous to the pests. Other insect pests spread bacteria that cause diseases by sucking the blood of sheep and cattle.

These adult migratory locusts are feeding on a corn plant. Locusts have a large head with short antennae, long back legs for jumping, and two pairs of wings.

Locusts live in warm countries where it doesn't rain very often. Every few years there may be more rain than usual. When this occurs, plants grow quickly, and more and more locusts survive because they have plenty to eat. Soon there are millions of locusts. They eat up all the food on the ground and fly off together in a huge swarm to look for even more food. Sometimes more than one billion insects join the swarm. A locust swarm may weigh as much as 300 elephants and eat more than 1,000 tons of crops and other plants in a day!

Aphids are tiny insects that are harmful to gardens, orchards, farm crops, and house plants. They feed on the sap of plants by pushing their tube-shaped mouths into the stems. If an aphid feeds on a diseased plant, it passes the disease on to the next plant it feeds on. Aphids live for only a short time, but they breed very quickly. Other insects, such as ladybirds, help the plants by eating the aphids.

This plant is covered, or infested, with aphids. When the colony of aphids gets too crowded, some of them grow wings and fly off to infest a new plant.

Make an aphid farm

Do **not** work near house plants.

You will need:

a saucer of water

a plant covered with aphids

a fine paintbrush

a magnifying glass

1. Cut a leaf without any aphids from the plant and float it upside down on the saucer of water.

2. Pick up a plump aphid from the plant with a fine paintbrush and put it on the floating leaf.

3. Later, look at the aphid through a magnifying glass and count how many babies have been born.

Extraordinary invertebrates

The world of invertebrates is full of animals with strange features or unusual habits. Let's look at the fierce weapons of two beetles and a shrimp—and let's discover a huge worm.

Bombardier beetle

Any animal that tried to attack a bombardier beetle would be in for a surprise. It defends itself by squirting two foul liquids from the end of its body. They mix together to produce a hot puff of gas that drives the beetle's enemies away.

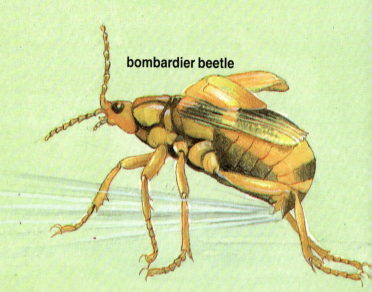

bombardier beetle

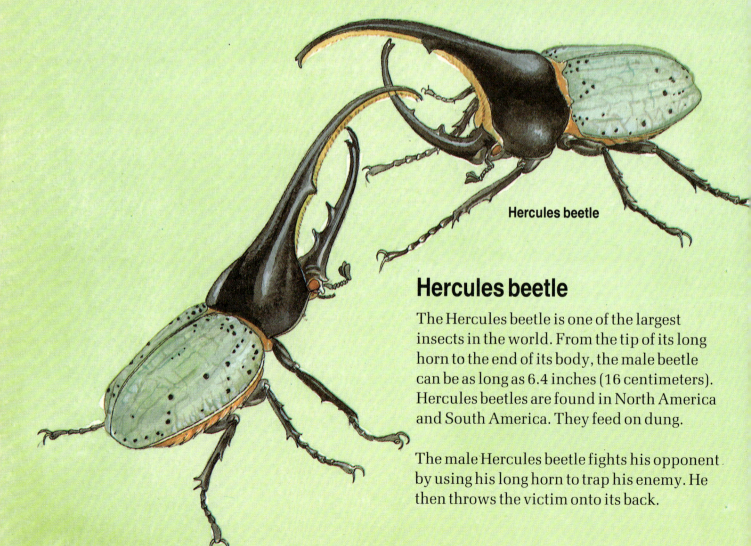

Hercules beetle

Hercules beetle

The Hercules beetle is one of the largest insects in the world. From the tip of its long horn to the end of its body, the male beetle can be as long as 6.4 inches (16 centimeters). Hercules beetles are found in North America and South America. They feed on dung.

The male Hercules beetle fights his opponent by using his long horn to trap his enemy. He then throws the victim onto its back.

Pistol shrimp

Hiding among sea anemones or corals may be a sharp-shooting shrimp! The pistol shrimp is about 2 inches (5 centimeters) long. When a small fish swims by, the shrimp aims its "pistol" and snaps together the pincers on the end of one of its claws. This sharp movement causes a shock wave in the water that stuns the fish just long enough for the shrimp to seize it. Then the shrimp kills and eats its victim.

Pistol shrimps use their claws to collect food and to fight their attackers.

Giant worm

Do you know what creature could live 1.8 miles (3 kilometers) under the sea, in the mouth of an underwater volcano? It is a giant worm 12 feet (3.5 meters) long and less than 1 inch (1.6 centimeters) wide.

Some scientists exploring the seabed near the Galapagos Islands in 1977 discovered some spouts of hot water 1.5 miles (2.5 kilometers) under the surface. The water there is full of strange chemicals, which are absorbed by millions of bacteria. Nearby the scientists found large colonies of giant worms. All these worms can get to eat are the bacteria around the volcano. But the worms have no mouth and no stomach! They absorb the bacteria through the thin skin of feathery tentacles that grow at one end of their bodies.

giant worm

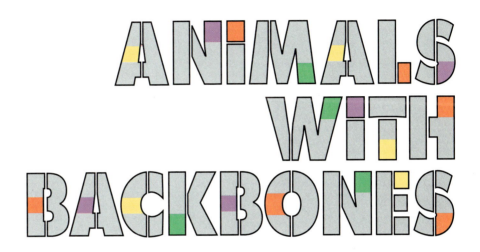

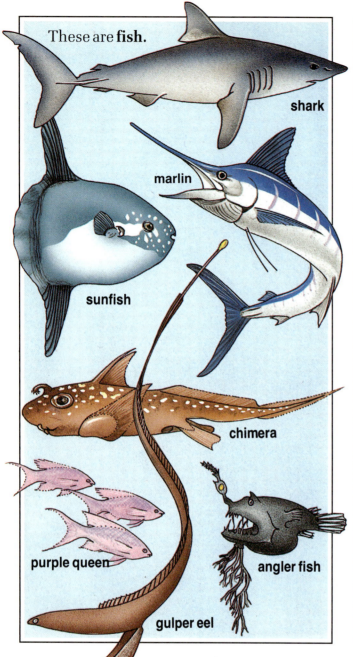

These are **fish**.

shark

marlin

sunfish

chimera

purple queen

gulper eel

angler fish

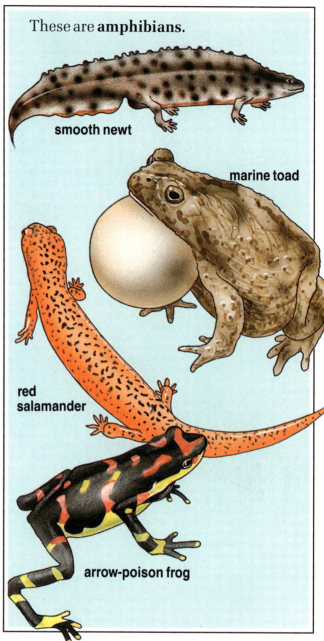

These are **amphibians**.

smooth newt

marine toad

red salamander

arrow-poison frog

These are vertebrates

What is a vertebrate? A **vertebrate** is an animal that has a **spinal column** (also called **spine** or backbone) and a **cranium** (brain case). Vertebrates can be divided into six groups, called classes—**cartilaginous fish, bony fish, amphibians, reptiles, birds,** and **mammals.** Each class has special characteristics. For example, birds have wings and feathers, most mammals have fur or hair, and the bones of cartilaginous fish are different from those of bony fish.

These are **reptiles**.

green turtle

ocellated green lizard

Asian wart snake

These are **birds**.

Eurasian kingfisher

toucan

Egyptian vulture

chaffinch

These are **mammals**.

African elephant

domestic cat

human

mouse

The vertebrates pictured here are not drawn to scale.

What is a fish?

Fish are vertebrates that live in water. They first appeared on the earth about 500 million years ago and were probably the first animals to have a backbone. Scientists have given names to nearly 22,000 different kinds, or **species,** of fish. They come in many different colors, shapes, and sizes. How many kinds of fish can you name?

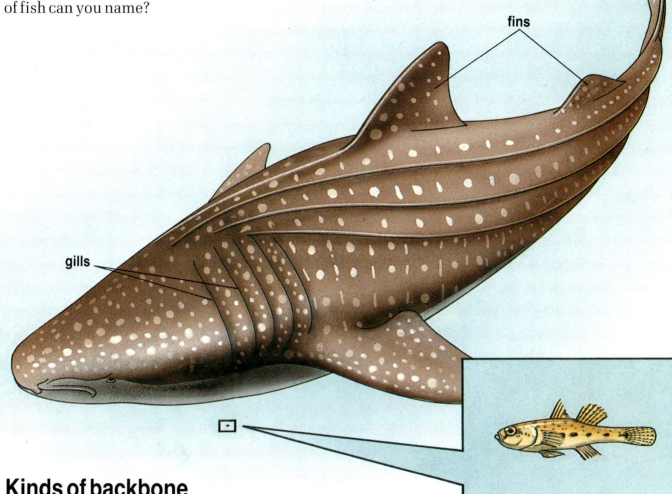

fins

gills

Kinds of backbone

Most fish have a spine, or backbone, made of hard bone which snaps if it's bent. These fish are called **bony fish.** Sharks and rays have a spine made of a tough, rubbery substance, called **cartilage,** which stretches like elastic. These fish are called **cartilaginous fish.**

Most fish breathe through a part of their body called **gills.** Gills enable fish to take in oxygen from the water. Most fish have skin covered with **scales.** These are thin, bony plates that form a protective covering. Nearly all fish have **fins** to help them swim. A fish uses its muscles to move its fins.

The smallest fish in the world is the pygmy goby. It lives in the Philippines and, when fully grown, is only ½ inch (13 millimeters) long. The world's largest fish is the whale shark, which may grow up to 60 feet (18 meters) in length.

The body of this porcupine fish is covered with sharp spines. When the fish inflates its body, the spines stick out. They protect the fish from danger.

Where do fish live?

More than half of all known species of fish live only in the sea. These are called **saltwater,** or **marine, fish.** The porcupine fish is a marine fish. Most other species of fish live only in fresh water—in lakes, rivers, and streams. The sturgeon is the largest kind of **freshwater fish.**

The salmon is an unusual fish because it spends part of its life in fresh water and part in salt water. Young salmon hatch in freshwater streams before swimming to the sea. Female salmon swim back to the stream where they were born to lay their eggs.

Did you know that some fish can survive out of water? The walking catfish can walk over land to reach water if its own stream or lake has dried up. It pushes itself along the ground with its tail and front fins. Most species of lungfish can live for months in dried-up riverbeds.

How old is a fish?

If you get a chance, try looking at some fish scales under a magnifying glass. Can you see some rings on them?

Every year, a new ring grows on a fish's scales. By counting the rings, you can tell how old the fish was when it was caught.

What is an amphibian?

An **amphibian** is a vertebrate that spends part of its life in water and part of its life on land. There are about 3,000 different species of amphibians. They include frogs, toads, newts, and salamanders.

When amphibians are young, they live in the water and breathe through gills, like fish. As they grow older, they develop **lungs** so they can survive on land.

Have you ever picked up an amphibian? Most amphibians have smooth skins. Toads have dry, rough skin covered with warts. Amphibians usually feel sticky to touch. A thick, slimy substance called **mucus** protects their skin and helps to keep it moist.

Amphibians' eggs are called **spawn.** These are soft and have no shell. The females of most frog and toad species lay hundreds of eggs at a time. Frogspawn is laid in a big mass, and toadspawn is laid in long strings. Female newts and salamanders lay their many eggs one at a time among underwater plants.

Salamanders live in streams and ponds, or in damp places on land.

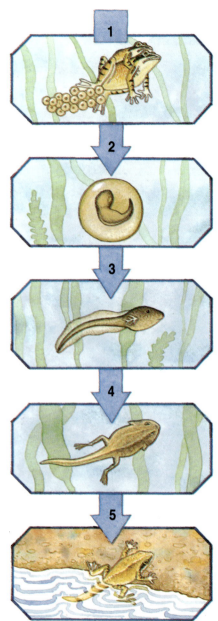

The life cycle of a frog begins when the female returns to a pond or stream to lay her eggs. The male frog clutches her sides and releases sperm on the eggs (1). Inside each fertilized egg a tiny tadpole grows (2) and then hatches out (3). After 8 weeks it has back legs (4), and after 12 weeks it has four legs but it still has some tail (5). Eventually, the tail is absorbed into the body.

You will need:

a small bucket

pond or stream water, stones, and underwater plants

some clean gravel

a stick or large rock

a small piece of meat on a string

a fish tank with a lid

Watch tadpoles grow up

1. Ask an adult to help you look for some frogspawn in a nearby stream or pond. Or perhaps your teacher can bring some to class. In your bucket, collect plants, stones, and water. Be careful when near the water's edge!

2. Now prepare your tank by covering the bottom of the tank with clean gravel. Fill the tank with pond water. Anchor the plants with stones. Put in the stick or large rock, so that later the young frogs can climb on it. Let the water settle for a day or two.

3. Carefully transfer the spawn into the tank. Watch the spawn every day. Within three weeks, tadpoles will hatch from the eggs. They grow the back legs first, then the front legs.

4. At first, tadpoles eat tiny plants. Once their back legs have grown, they will eat a small piece of meat hung in the tank. After a couple of hours, remove the string.

5. When the young frogs start climbing out of the water onto the stick or rock, take them back to the pond or stream where they came from, and let them go.

Did you notice that frogs lose their tadpole tails? Because they spend more time on land, they don't need their tails. Adult newts and salamanders spend much more time in the water. They need their tails to help them swim.

This egg-eating snake swallows an egg whole, then crushes it inside its throat before spitting out the eggshell.

What is a reptile?

Lizards and snakes, crocodiles and alligators, turtles and tortoises—all these vertebrates are **reptiles.** They have dry skin covered with scales. They breathe air through lungs, and most species lay their eggs on land. The eggs of some reptiles have leathery shells. Others are hard, like birds' eggs.

Lizards and snakes

There are nearly 3,000 different species of **lizards.** Lizards like to live in hot places. A lizard can survive the heat of the desert because its scaly skin keeps the moisture inside its body. Most lizards have eyelids that close, ears on their head, a long tail, and four legs. A few lizards, such as "glass snakes" and slow worms, have no legs.

There are almost as many species of **snakes** as there are species of lizards. Snakes have no legs and no eyelids, and their ears are inside their head. Their eyes are protected by transparent scales. Most snakes live in warm places, but some can live in colder climates. Most snakes swallow their prey—including frogs, rats, fish, and birds—alive.

common wall lizard

The crocodilians

Alligators and crocodiles belong to a group of reptiles called **crocodilians.** They all live in or near water. Most live in tropical countries, either in freshwater rivers and lakes, or in the low-lying areas nearby. Crocodilians have long snouts, strong jaws and webbed back feet. Small crocodiles eat fish but bigger ones can eat quite large animals, including turtles. A big crocodile can kill a human being with one lash of its tail!

Some reptiles have shells

Turtles and tortoises are the only reptiles with shells. They belong to a group known as **chelonians.** Turtles live on land, in fresh water, or in the ocean. Tortoises live only on land. Many turtles live for a very long time — some have survived for as long as 150 years! Female chelonians dig a hole in the mud or sand. Here, they lay their eggs, cover them and leave them alone to hatch. When the young hatch, they dig their way out and search for food.

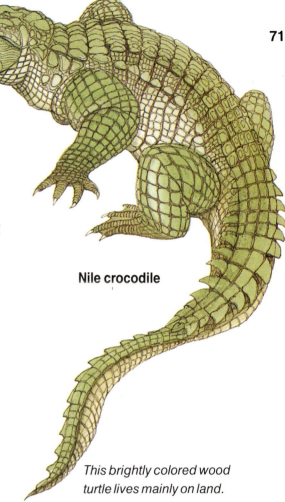

Nile crocodile

This brightly colored wood turtle lives mainly on land.

Find out more by looking at pages **82–83**

What is a bird?

Wherever you go in the world, you will see birds. Scientists have named about 8,600 different species of bird. Some species live in forests, while others live on grasslands, in deserts, on mountaintops or on uninhabited islands. Some live near human beings — around farmlands and in cities. **Birds** are the only animals with feathers. All birds have wings but not all of them can fly. A flying bird can travel faster than any other animal.

Feeding and flying

The kind of food that birds eat varies from one group of birds to another.

barn owl

golden swallow

hummingbird

Hummingbirds are tiny birds that feed on nectar from flowers. They have a long, slender beak and a long tongue. Hummingbirds are skillful fliers and can hover in front of a flower for several minutes. Some can even fly backward!

Birds of prey, such as eagles and hawks, catch mice, lizards, snakes, and other small animals. Some even catch fish. The bald eagle uses its claws to snatch fish from the water while flying. Birds of prey have sharp, curved beaks that can tear flesh. Owls hunt at night and catch farm pests like rats and mice.

Swallows, martins, and swifts have large mouths adapted to catching flying insects. Their long, curved wings help them to fly fast, and to twist and turn in the air.

Ostriches are the largest living birds. Sometimes, they grow as tall as 8 feet (2.4 meters). An ostrich is too big to fly, but it can run as fast as 40 miles (64 kilometers) an hour, using its wings to balance itself.

penguins

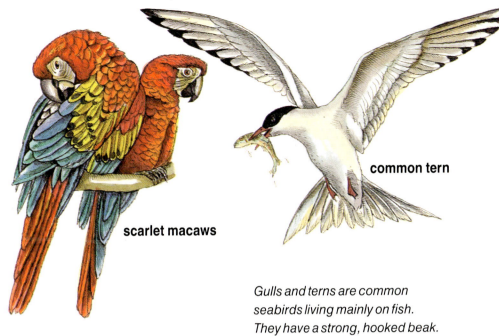

scarlet macaws

common tern

Gulls and terns are common
seabirds living mainly on fish.
They have a strong, hooked beak.

*Penguins lost the ability to fly
millions of years ago. They use their
wings as flippers for swimming in
the water. On land, penguins walk
or slide along.*

*Macaws live in the forested areas
of Central and South America. They
eat nuts, seeds and fruit, using a
short, arched beak.*

The birds are not drawn to scale.

How do birds breed?

All birds hatch from eggs. Usually, the
female lays her eggs in a nest built by herself
or her mate, or both. Baby birds may stay
in the nest for weeks after hatching.
The parent birds feed and protect the
young birds until they can look after
themselves.

hummingbird's nest

osprey

grouse

Baltimore oriole

marsh warbler

74

What is a mammal?

You are a mammal. Cats and dogs, goats and horses, apes and monkeys, giraffes and elephants, even whales and dolphins are all mammals. There are about 4,000 different species of mammals. What do they all have in common?

Mammals, like other vertebrates, produce eggs. But most of them don't lay the eggs and wait for them to hatch. Instead, the mother keeps the eggs inside her body and the young grow inside her until they are ready to be born. After birth, the mother feeds her young on milk she has produced herself.

Most mammals are covered with fur, hair, or bristles. Some mammals, such as elephants, have very little hair. Our ancestors had thick hair all over their bodies. Today, human beings have thick hair on only some parts of their bodies.

Mammals and their young

Scientists can sort, or **classify,** mammals into smaller groups by looking at the ways they produce their young and care for them. Using this method, scientists have sorted mammals into three groups—placentals, marsupials, and monotremes.

The blue whale is the largest animal that ever lived. An adult blue whale can measure as long as 100 feet (30 meters). It weighs about 190 tons. An adult giraffe can grow to be about 18 feet (5 meters) tall. An Indian bull elephant weighs nearly 4 tons.

giraffe Indian elephant

blue whale

Placentals

Humans, and most other mammals, belong to the **placentals** group. Before they are born, placental mammals develop inside the mother. They are attached to their mother by a cord, or **placenta,** through which they get their food. Newborn placentals are already well developed. Have you ever seen a newborn calf or foal? Most can stand after only a few minutes. Newborn whales can swim at once. Human babies are still quite helpless.

Marsupials

Kangaroos, possums, wombats and koalas are **marsupials.** Most marsupials live in Australia. These mammals give birth to tiny young that don't look a bit like their parents. These tiny creatures wiggle their way through their mother's fur and into a pouch below her stomach. Here, they feed on milk until they are big enough to leave. Whenever they are in danger, they return to the pouch.

A young wallaby stays in its mother's pouch for several months after its birth. This fat-tailed swamp wallaby and her baby live in the east and south of Australia. Wallabies are smaller members of the kangaroo family.

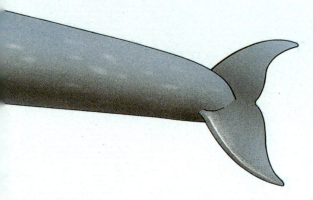

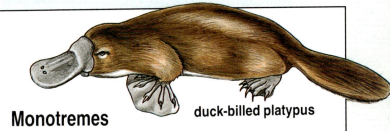

duck-billed platypus

Monotremes

The third group of mammals—the **monotremes**—all live in Australia or on islands nearby. There are only three species of monotremes—one species is the duck-billed platypus. The other two are different species of spiny anteaters. Monotremes are classed as mammals because the mothers produce milk. But their young aren't born like other mammals. They hatch out of eggs.

What is a backbone?

Animals that are vertebrates have a spine, or backbone, and a cranium (brain case). The spine is a long column of bones called **vertebrae** that run all the way along an animal's back. Most vertebrates have vertebrae made of bones. Some, like sharks, have vertebrae of cartilage

You can feel your vertebrae by running your hand down the back of your neck and between your shoulder blades. Can you feel a row of hard, bony lumps? They run all the way down to your bottom.

What does the backbone do?

The backbone has a very important job to do. Every vertebra that makes up the backbone has a hole in the middle, and is joined to the next by a rubbery pad of cartilage. The backbone is like a flexible, hollow tube. Through the middle of this tube runs the spinal cord.

The **spinal cord** is a thick bundle of nerves that carries messages from a vertebrate's brain to the rest of its body. The spinal cord also carries information back from the body to the brain. The backbone protects this vital passageway of nerves.

Every animal in the six classes of vertebrates—bony fish, cartilaginous fish, amphibians, reptiles, birds, and mammals—has a spine, or backbone.

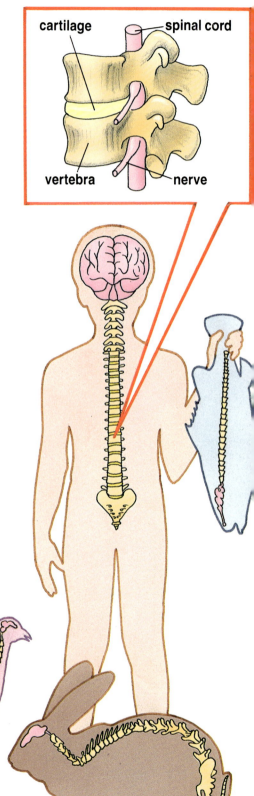

cartilage · spinal cord

vertebra · nerve

Reacting to pain

If you dip your foot into hot water, messages will race through your spinal cord and to your brain to say that the water is too hot and that it's causing you pain. Messages will then race back to your leg muscles to take your foot out of the water.

Imagine how busy the nerves in your backbone are! Thousands of messages rush along them every second. If the spinal cord gets damaged, these messages can't get through. Sometimes, people who have injured their back can't move certain parts of their body.

Messages travel rapidly along the nerves between your foot, spinal cord, and brain. When the water is too hot, you quickly lift up your leg. Your brain then receives a signal that the foot is now out of the water.

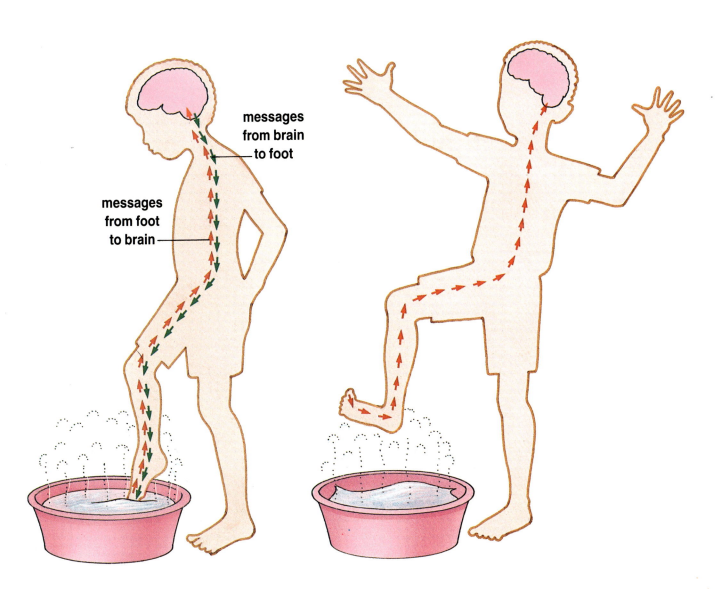

messages from brain to foot

messages from foot to brain

What is a skeleton?

Over many thousands of years, most vertebrates have developed a bony structure inside their body called a **skeleton.** The skeleton includes the backbone.

The skeleton makes a framework which supports the vertebrate's body and affects the way it moves. Some vertebrates have arms, some have legs, some have wings, and some have flippers. Their limbs have developed in different ways. Snakes have no legs. Another reptile, the two-legged worm lizard, has two tiny but powerful front legs. Other species of worm lizard have no legs at all.

Arms, legs, wings and tails

These skeletons are not drawn to scale.

whale skeleton

The skeletons of some whales still have bones which show where back legs used to grow. Sometimes, whales have been found with tiny pairs of hind legs. Their front legs have become flippers, which they use for swimming.

bat skeleton

The front legs of a bat have developed into wings made of a thick membrane. When they roost, bats hang upside down by their feet. Birds have wings covered in feathers. These have developed from the front legs of the dinosaurs.

mole skeleton

A mole has wide, spade-like arms with heavy bones. It uses these arms to dig through the earth. A mole's skull is long and tapered at the front, for pushing through the soil.

Mexican worm lizard

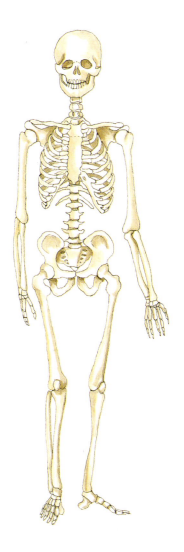

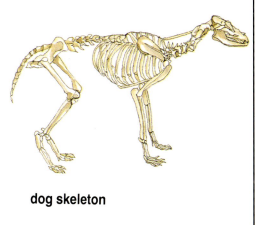

dog skeleton

The dog has long legs underneath its body, for running after its prey.

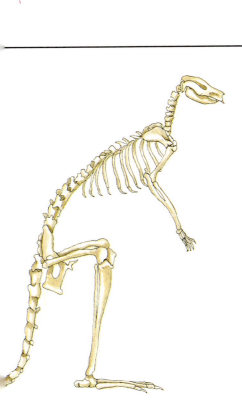

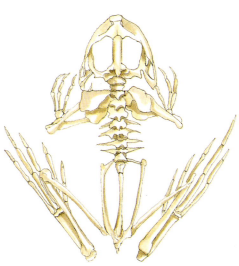

human skeleton

Human beings have hands for holding and making things. These developed when the front pair of legs gradually became a pair of arms, with hands instead of feet. Because human beings don't have a tail as a counterbalance, we have to be upright in order to balance ourselves while walking.

kangaroo skeleton

Kangaroos have powerful back legs, short front arms, and a strong tail. A kangaroo can hop on its back legs at a speed of up to 40 miles (64 kilometers) per hour. A kangaroo uses its long, muscular tail for balance when it hops.

frog skeleton

A frog's short, stiff backbone provides strength when the frog is jumping and landing. The frog doesn't have a tail, which might get in the way when it jumps, but it does have long legs.

Prehistoric vertebrates

Many of the animals that lived millions of years ago, during what are called **prehistoric times,** looked very different from the animals that live in our world today.

The earliest vertebrates that we know existed were species of fish. The cephalaspid, for example, lived about 400 million years ago, when most of the earth was still covered by water. Then, as the sea level dropped, more land appeared. Some animals, such as the ichthyostega and the diplocaulus, were able to live both in and out of the water. The legs of these early amphibians were set at the sides of their body. They walked clumsily, their stomach nearly touching the ground.

Giant reptiles

Giant reptiles called dinosaurs, such as triceratops, stegosaurus, and tyrannosaurus rex, dominated the world between 240 and 63 million years ago. The legs of these reptiles were straight, and set underneath their body. They could move about quickly and easily.

The pteranodon was a reptile that could fly, even without feathers. And scientists have found fossils of a bird called the archaeopteryx, which had feathers and reptile features. These first birds were only about 18 inches (46 centimeters) long.

The jawless cephalaspid was one of the oldest known fishes. Around its head was a protective plate shaped like a triangular shield.

Tyrannosaurus rex was a meat-eating dinosaur. It grew to be about 40 feet (12 meters) long and had teeth 6 inches (15 centimeters) long. It was probably one of the fiercest dinosaurs of its period.

Pteranodon was a flying reptile with huge, bat-like wings. It had claws on top of its wings and a horn-like crest on the back of its head. Its wingspan was about 26 feet (8 meters).

Extinction

About 63 million years ago, the giant reptiles became **extinct,** or died out. Many scientists believe that the world became a very cold place around this time. The giant reptiles died because they had no fur or feathers to keep them warm and were too big to hibernate. **Hibernation** is an inactive, sleeplike state that protects animals against the cold and reduces the need for food. Scientists know what these animals looked like by examining **fossils.** These are either skeletons or the impressions formed by the crushed bodies of dead animals in very old rocks.

You will need:

modeling clay

at least eight matchsticks

coins

Straight legs are strong legs

1. Make two clay bodies, each about two inches (5 centimeters) long and the same shape and size.

Bend four of the matchsticks about one-third of the way down. Be careful not to break them.

2. Push the bent matchsticks into the sides of one of the clay bodies to make an amphibian.

Push four straight matchsticks into the bottom of the other clay body to make a reptile. Put the models in a cool place so that the clay hardens.

3. Add an equal number of coins to the back of each model, one coin at a time. Which model collapses first? Do you know why it does?

Find out more by looking at
pages **72–73**
   80–81

How do birds fly?

One group of dinosaurs grew feathers, learned to fly, and still lives all around us today. Which group of vertebrates is this?

Most scientists believe that birds are descended from reptiles, because their skeletons look similar. Scientists have found fossils of a very old bird that resembled reptiles in many ways. They call it archaeopteryx.

Many of the birds we see flying today weigh much less than creatures like archaeopteryx. Over thousands of years, they have lost their jaws and teeth, and developed a beak instead. They have long tail feathers instead of a long, bony tail, and hollow bones, which make them lighter still.

Looking at feathers

Birds have three kinds of feathers. **Down feathers** are the smallest and the first to grow. They have a central shaft, with thinner, fluffy strands called **barbs** on either side. Many birds have down over much of their bodies to keep them warm.

Flight feathers are made up of a long, hollow shaft. The barbs on either side are held together by hundreds of tiny hooks. Rub the barbs of a flight feather down the shaft and back up again. The strands join together like hundreds of tiny zippers! **Semiplumes,** or body feathers, are smaller and fluffier than flight feathers, and are usually covered by them.

semiplume

down feather

flight feather

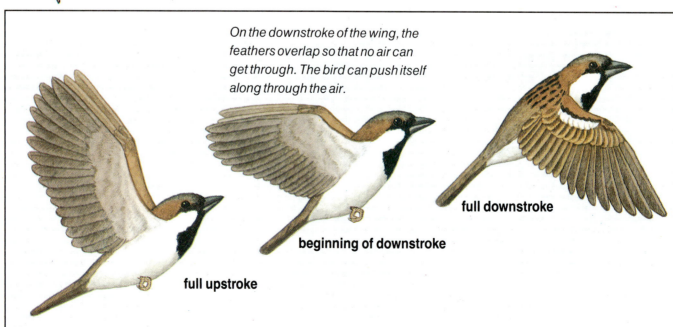

On the downstroke of the wing, the feathers overlap so that no air can get through. The bird can push itself along through the air.

full downstroke

beginning of downstroke

full upstroke

Collecting feathers

You will need:

a notebook

a pencil

scissors

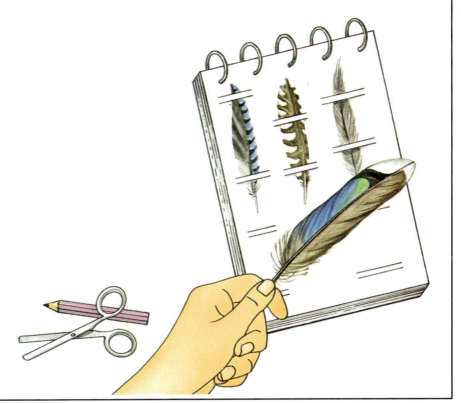

1. Collect feathers and fix them in a notebook. Feathers keep birds warm, help them to fly, and even act as a raincoat.

2. Look at all the different types of feathers. Do you know which bird they belong to?

Remember to wash your hands after handling feathers.

Watching birds fly

Birds flap their wings most of the time as they launch themselves into the air. Many smaller birds continue to flap their wings as they fly. Some larger birds can glide or soar with little flapping of the wings.

beginning of upstroke

On the upstroke, the feathers twist open so air passes through, allowing the bird to lift its wings easily.

pheasant

gull

swift

The pheasant can take off quickly but flies fast only a short distance. The swift is a fast flier. The gull is best at soaring and gliding. How do you think the shape of the wings affects the ways each of these birds flies?

How do fish swim?

Most fish swim by waving their tails from side to side. Some fish, such as plaice and flounders, are flat. When these fish swim, they move up and down. Eels are fish with long bodies. An eel swims by moving its whole body from side to side.

By moving certain fins, fish can change direction. They can go up or down, from left to right, or from right to left.

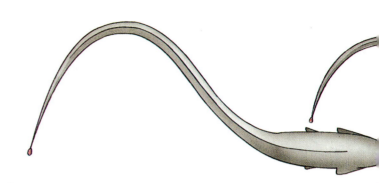

Make a model fish

You will need:

small rubber bands

some stiff plastic or polystyrene

scissors

a stapler or paper clips

a large bowl of water

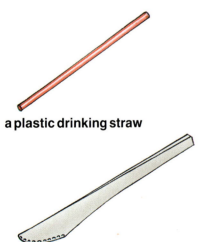

a balloon

a plastic drinking straw

a plastic knife

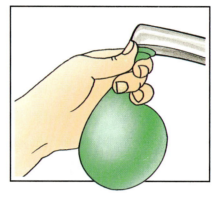

1. Hold the balloon over the end of a faucet, and fill it halfway with water. Remove the balloon from the tap, holding the neck tightly.

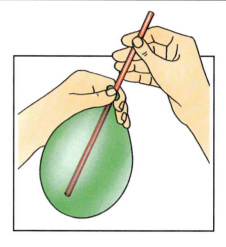

2. Over a sink, open the balloon a little, and push the straw right down inside. Some water may spill out, but if you do this quickly you won't lose too much.

3. Grip the neck of the balloon tightly. Fasten the neck to the straw with a rubber band.

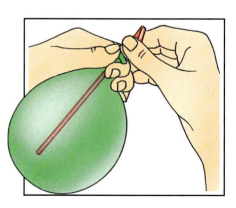

4. Fold the straw over and use another rubber band on the straw to keep the end folded over.

Eels, such as this gulper fish, swim by bending their body into snake-like curves.

Find out more by looking at pages **66 – 67**

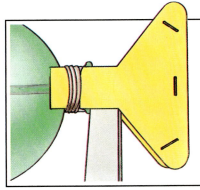

5. Now cut out two tail-shaped pieces from your stiff plastic. Put one against each side of the balloon neck and hold them in place with rubber bands. Use staples or paper clips to hold the outer edges of the tail together.

6. Push the plastic knife upright between the two halves of the tail, and put your fish into the bowl of water. You are ready to see how a fish swims.

7. Press one finger lightly against the "nose" of your fish, just enough to stop it from moving side to side. Now push the tail from side to side using the plastic knife. The fish will "swim" through the water.

Find out more by looking at
pages **66–67**
106–107

Vertebrates need oxygen

Vertebrates, including human beings, have to breathe continuously, all day and all night. They breathe even when they are asleep. When we breathe air in, we take in a gas called oxygen. When we breathe out, we release a gas called carbon dioxide. Biologists call this process **exchanging gases.** Every vertebrate needs to exchange oxygen for carbon dioxide in order to stay alive.

Taking in oxygen

Oxygen is mixed with other gases in the air around us. It is also dissolved in water. Mammals, birds and reptiles take in oxygen from the air through their lungs. Fish use their gills to take in the oxygen that is dissolved in water. Some adult amphibians, such as mudpuppies, have lungs and gills! These amphibians can breathe both on land and in the water. Amphibians also take in some of the oxygen they need through their skin.

Oxygen gets into the blood through millions of tiny blood vessels around the gills or lungs. Blood contains a substance called **hemoglobin** that soaks up oxygen like a sponge. Blood carries oxygen from the lungs to all parts of the body, and brings back carbon dioxide to be breathed out.

Most fish breathe with gills, which are placed on each side of the fish's body just behind the head. Water flows through the fish's mouth, over the gills, and back out again. As the water flows through the gills, capillaries absorb oxygen and expel carbon dioxide.

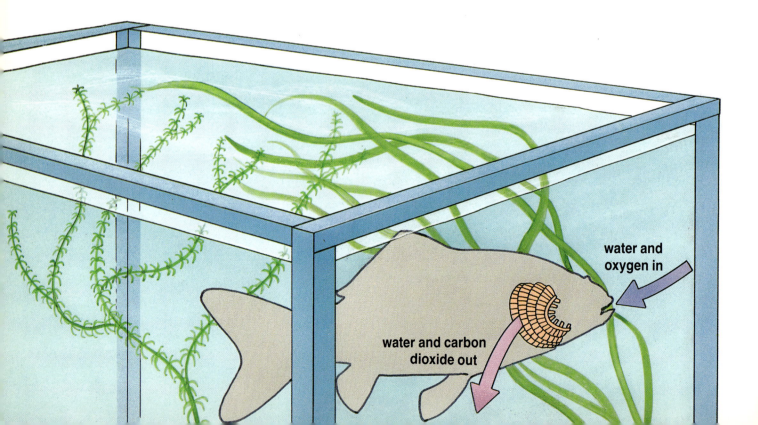

water and oxygen in

water and carbon dioxide out

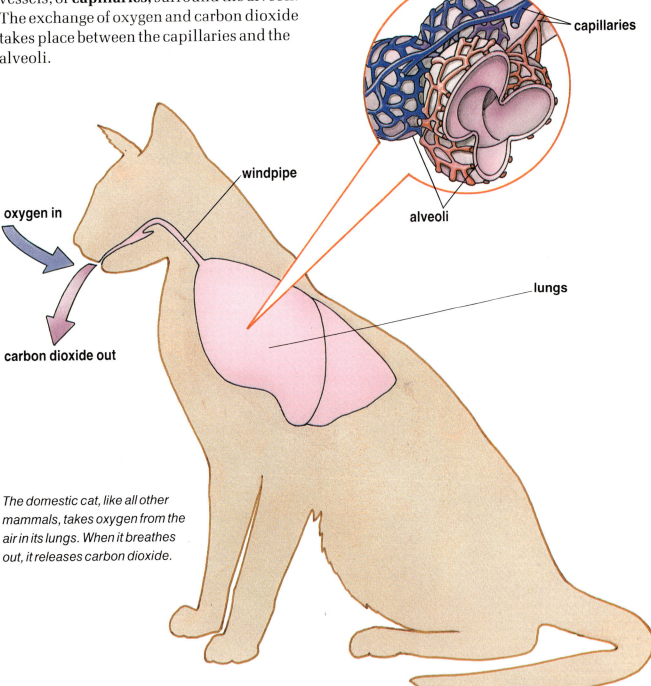

Inside vertebrate lungs

Your windpipe divides into two trunk-like shapes called **bronchi,** one leading to the left lung, and the other to the right lung. Each **bronchus** divides and subdivides into smaller "branches" called **bronchioles.** At the end of the smallest bronchioles are hollow pouches, called **alveoli.** Tiny blood vessels, or **capillaries,** surround the alveoli. The exchange of oxygen and carbon dioxide takes place between the capillaries and the alveoli.

This shows a close-up view of the inside of a cat's lung. The alveoli are surrounded by capillaries. The side of one of the alveoli has been cut away.

bronchiole

capillaries

alveoli

windpipe

oxygen in

carbon dioxide out

lungs

The domestic cat, like all other mammals, takes oxygen from the air in its lungs. When it breathes out, it releases carbon dioxide.

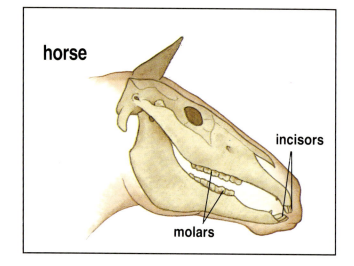

horse

incisors

molars

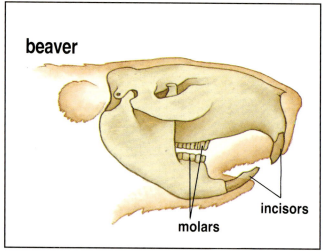

beaver

incisors

molars

These drawings of the jaws of four different mammals show the three kinds of mammal teeth—incisors, canines and molars.

These jaws are not drawn to scale.

What do mammals eat?

These jaws belong to different mammals. Look at the teeth. Most mammals have some sharp teeth at the front, called **incisors,** and some blunter, more rounded teeth at the sides, called **molars.** Some mammals also have sharp, pointed teeth called **canines.** You can tell what kind of food a mammal eats by looking at the shape and position of its teeth. It will eat either plants, or the flesh of other animals, or both. A few mammals eat only insects. They have unusual teeth or none at all.

Mammals can be grouped, or classified, by the kind of food they eat. The kind of food is related to the kind and placement of the teeth.

Plant eaters

Most mammals are herbivores. **Herbivores** eat plants. Cattle, horses and sheep are herbivores that eat grasses. Most of their teeth are at the side, inside their cheeks. Watch a herbivore eating grass. It pulls up the grass with its incisors, then grinds it up with its strong molars.

Beavers, rats and squirrels belong to a smaller group of herbivores called rodents. **Rodents** gnaw their food. They have very large incisors for tearing bark from trees, or shells off nuts. Their front teeth never stop growing, so despite all the chewing, the teeth are never worn down.

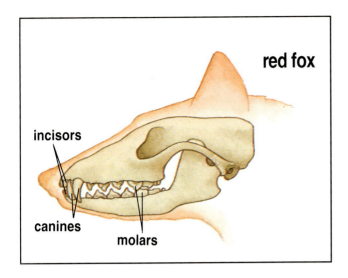

red fox

incisors

canines

molars

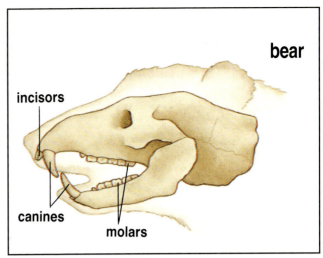

bear

incisors

canines

molars

Meat eaters

Some mammals are carnivores. **Carnivores** eat the flesh of other animals. A carnivore has teeth all around the front of its mouth. Some carnivores, like lions and foxes, use their incisors and canine teeth to stab and hold their prey. Then they crush the meat and bones with their molars.

Plant and meat eaters

Mammals that are **omnivores** eat both plants and animals. Human beings are omnivores. So are bears and animals like hogs and opossums. Omnivores have teeth all around the front of their mouth—incisors for biting and cutting, canines for tearing meat, and close-set molars for chewing plants.

Insect eaters

Animals that eat mainly insects are called **insectivores.** Anteaters and hedgehogs are insectivores. Some insectivores have weak teeth, and some don't have any at all. They lick up ants and termites with their long, sticky tongues.

The giant anteater of South America eats only ants and termites. Its tongue, which can be as long as 2 feet (60 centimeters), is covered with a sticky substance so that the insects stick to it.

Extraordinary vertebrates

Among the thousands of different kinds of vertebrates, there are some which look strange and others which behave in unusual ways. The thorny devil, for example, looks different from most other lizards. The long-nosed bandicoot, unlike some other marsupials, has a backward-facing pouch.

sea horse

Sea horses are very strange fish. They swim along in an upright position, propelled by rapid movements of the fin on their back. When one wants to stay in one place, it wraps its tail around some seaweed!

Female sea horses lay as many as 200 eggs at a time. The male sea horse carries these eggs in a pouch on the underside of his body until they hatch.

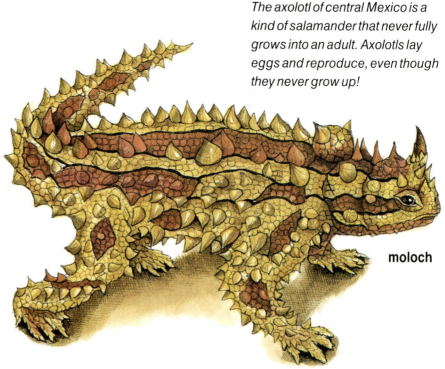

The axolotl of central Mexico is a kind of salamander that never fully grows into an adult. Axolotls lay eggs and reproduce, even though they never grow up!

The Australian moloch, or thorny devil, has a body completely covered from head to tail in short, thorn-like spines. Although it looks frightening, it cannot move very fast. Newly hatched molochs look just like fully grown ones, only smaller!

moloch

Long-nosed bandicoots are Australian marsupials that keep their young in a pouch, like a kangaroo. But the bandicoot's pouch faces backward, not forward like the kangaroo's pouch. Thus when the mother bandicoot burrows in the earth, the soil she digs up can't get into the pouch and suffocate her young.

long-nosed bandicoot

giraffes

Believe it or not, giraffes in Africa have the same number of vertebrae in their neck as human beings — seven. A baby giraffe is called a calf and can stand up just one hour after being born.

Giraffes sleep standing up. They never kneel down. When a giraffe wants to drink, it spreads its forelegs until its head can reach the water.

Sleeping and waking

Every night, while you are asleep, your body is resting. While your body rests, your brain and nervous system get back some of the energy you have used up during the day.

Most animals rest by sleeping. Some animals close their eyes and curl up while the sleep, but many animals don't look as though they are sleeping at all.

Cattle, horses, and giraffes can sleep standing up. Sleeping birds usually have one eye open to watch for danger. And some swifts may actually doze off in the air for a few minutes at a time, as they are flying.

Dolphins and whales can't fall asleep completely because they have to keep swimming to the surface of the sea to breathe. Scientists have discovered that one half of a dolphin's brain sleeps while the other half stays awake. The two halves of the brain take turns in having a rest!

dunlins

white-lipped peccaries

red kangaroos

lion

red panda

grey heron

Do animals dream?

Scientists can tell when mammals, birds, and reptiles go to sleep. All animals produce electrical waves from their brain. These waves form a certain pattern when the animal is awake. But when the animal falls asleep, the wave pattern changes. If the animal is dreaming, the pattern changes again.

By looking at these changing patterns of **brain waves,** scientists have discovered that all mammals have dreams. Birds have only short dreams. Most reptiles don't dream at all, and neither do fish or amphibians.

Fish never close their eyes, but they sometimes seem to take less notice of what is happening around them than normal. You might say they were asleep, but you couldn't be sure!

Sleeping during the cold season

In those parts of the world where some months of the year are very cold, mice and other small mammals **hibernate.** This means that they go into an inactive, sleeplike state for the cold period and only fully wake up when the weather turns warm again.

Hibernating animals breathe much more slowly and their body temperature falls. They also need much less food. They build up a thick layer of fat during the warmer months and use it up very slowly during hibernation.

A dormouse can sleep in its nest for up to nine months in a year. It may wake up at intervals during this time to nibble at its store of nuts and berries.

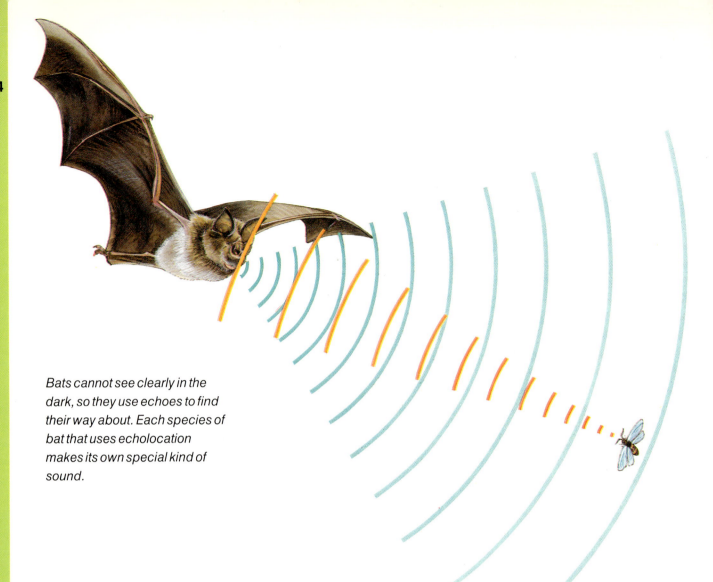

Bats cannot see clearly in the dark, so they use echoes to find their way about. Each species of bat that uses echolocation makes its own special kind of sound.

Vertebrate senses

How do you find out about the world around you? You do this by using your five senses. You can see, hear, smell, touch, and taste. Animals also have senses to help them find out about the world.

A sense of hearing

Hearing is very important to bats. Some bats have a sense that is like the radar used in aircraft. These bats make sound signals that bounce back if they hit a solid object, such as a wall, a tree, or the insects on which these bats feed. Sounds bouncing back are called **echoes.** The pattern of echoes helps the bats to make up a picture of their surroundings. This method of finding out what is around them is called **echolocation.**

Dogs, cats, and fish

Dogs have a very good sense of smell that helps them find food and follow tracks.

Cats have long, sensitive whiskers to help them feel their way around at night without bumping into things.

Fish can feel movement in the water through a sense system called a **lateral line.** The messages a fish's brain receives through this line let it know the position of animals and objects it can't see.

How a bat finds its way about

1. Use a sheet of foil to make a tray about 14 inches (35 centimeters) wide. Fold the edges of the foil up and over twice to make the sides of the tray.

2. Use the modeling clay to make a wall with flat sides about 5 inches (12.5 centimeters) long. Place the wall in the tray about 4 inches (10 centimeters) in from the end farthest from you.

3. Place the tray on a flat surface with a light shining onto it from the far end. Make sure the source of light is low down. Fill the tray with water to a depth of about .2 inch (5 millimeters). Be very careful not to burn yourself on the light bulb. And don't splash water onto the lamp!

Push out the sides of the tray until they are sloping and the water almost starts to spill over.

4. With one fingertip, touch the surface of the water at the near end of the tray. Then lift your finger and watch the ripple flow away in all directions.

5. Do you see the ripples coming back from the wall toward you? These small waves in the water are like the echoes of sound returning from nearby objects that tell a bat where the objects are.

You will need:

aluminum foil

water

modeling clay

a lamp

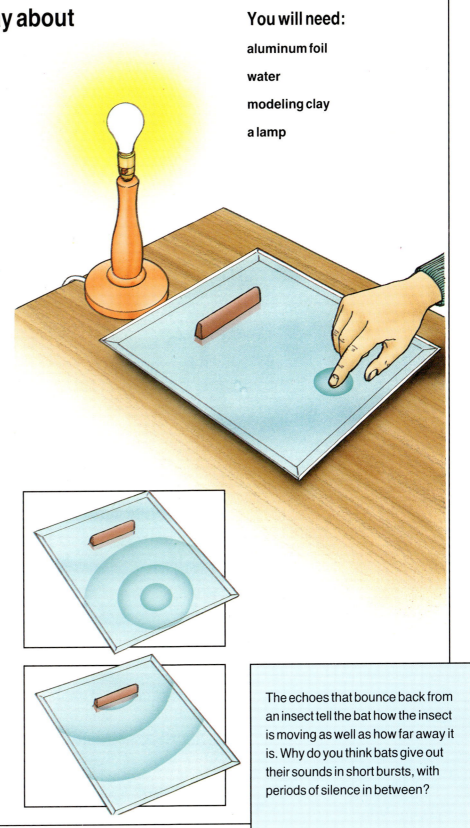

The echoes that bounce back from an insect tell the bat how the insect is moving as well as how far away it is. Why do you think bats give out their sounds in short bursts, with periods of silence in between?

Animal travelers

What do you do when it's cold outside and you are feeling hungry? You go indoors where it's warm and you can find food. When animals are cold or hungry, they move to warmer places where they can find food more easily.

Some animals travel very long distances to find warmth and food, or to give birth to their young. They sometimes travel in large groups. We say that these animals **migrate,** and we call their journeys **migrations.**

common eel

Some eels swim more than 4,340 miles (7,000 kilometers) from Europe and Eastern North America to the Sargasso Sea in the Atlantic. After the eels lay their eggs, they die. The young eels swim to Europe and North America, where they live for up to 10 years in rivers before returning to the Sargasso.

Arctic tern

Arctic terns fly a round trip of more than 21,700 miles (35,000 kilometers) every year, from one end of the earth to the other. No other bird travels as far as this tern. The terns nest around the North Pole in June and July, which are the warmer months. Then they migrate to the South Pole, where December and January are the warmer months and where food is easier to find.

barn swallow

Some smaller birds, such as warblers and swallows, live in Europe during the warmer months. When it grows cold there, these birds fly south to the warmth of Africa.

ruff

The ruff breeds in countries north of the equator, especially in the Arctic regions, before making the journey south to its feeding grounds.

This map shows some of the longest migration routes undertaken by different animals, across land and sea and through the air.

The arrows show the route from the breeding grounds to the feeding places.

grey whale

The grey whale may travel more than 12,400 miles (20,000 kilometers) from the areas where it breeds to the Arctic waters where there is plenty of food.

blue wildebeest

Some mammals, including African elephants and wildebeest and American caribou, migrate regularly over land.

needle-tailed swift

The needle-tailed swift of Asia is one of the fastest-flying birds.

Find out more by looking at
pages **68–69**
72–73
104–105

Animal defenses

The world is a dangerous place for most animals. Many need to defend themselves against other animals that want to eat them. An animal that is hunted, killed, and eaten by another is called **prey.** Animals that hunt prey are called **predators.**

Some animals are able to disguise, or **camouflage,** themselves as a protection against predators. But there are many other ways in which an animal can defend itself.

One species of lizard, the leaf-tailed gecko of Australia, has a tail that looks like its head! You can imagine how confusing this must be for the lizard's enemies. If a predator grabs this gecko by the tail, the tail breaks off, and the gecko can escape. Later, a new tail will grow.

Birds that nest on the ground are usually camouflaged. Goatsuckers (also known as nightjars) and whippoorwills look like a pile of dead leaves. Ringed plovers look like the pebbles on the beaches where they nest.

goatsucker

green chameleon

tiger

Camouflage can help some predators to get near their prey without being seen. The tiger's stripes help it to blend in with the tall grasses of its hunting ground. Polar bears have white fur to match the surrounding snow.

A certain group of lizards, called chameleons, can change the shading of their skin color to match their surroundings and confuse their enemies. For example, green chameleons can change from light green to dark green.

Protection from danger

Some animals, including opossums and snakes, pretend to be dead when they are in danger. Most predators prefer live prey, so they leave the "dead" animal alone. Other snakes defend themselves with poisonous bites.

Armadillos and pangolins are two species of animals that roll up into a ball when in danger. This protects the soft undersides of their bodies. Both animals have a thick coat of armor made of bony plates on the outside of their bodies. When predators come close, porcupines and hedgehogs might also defend themselves by rolling up into a ball. Such a ball of needle-sharp quills scares away many predators.

Indian pangolin

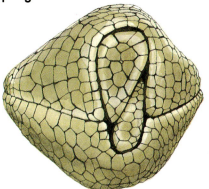

Porcupines have a painful and effective way of dealing with predators. They have spines called **quills,** that drop out easily. When a porcupine is threatened, it may run backward toward its enemy. Quills get stuck in the predator's nose and face or other part of the body, giving the porcupine a chance to run away.

arrow-poison frog

When the prickly puffer fish is frightened, it can blow itself up to twice its normal size. Most predators don't want to eat a prickly balloon. Its flesh is usually poisonous, too!

African porcupine

puffer fish

The skin of animals that are poisonous to eat is often brightly colored. The bright colors of the arrow-poison frogs of South America warn predators to keep away! Some salamanders ooze poisons from their skin when they are in danger.

Seals have a layer of fat, or blubber, around their bodies. The blubber can be as much as 6 inches (15 centimeters) thick. It helps the seal to stay warm and gives the seal energy when it has no food.

Keeping warm and staying cool

Some animals are able to keep themselves warm in cold weather. Other animals cannot do this, so they have to move to a warmer place or hibernate.

Keeping warm

Animals which can keep themselves warm are described as **warm-blooded.** Whatever the weather, they maintain a steady body temperature. All mammals and birds are warm-blooded. Their bodies make heat by burning up some of the food they eat. Some mammals have fur and birds have feathers to help keep in the heat. Whales and dolphins have a thick layer of fat, called **blubber,** to keep them warm. Some seals have a thick layer of fat and a thin coat of fur as well.

Cold-blooded animals have to move between warm and cool places to control their body temperature. All fish, amphibians, and reptiles are cold-blooded. When they are in a hot place, they can get very warm indeed!

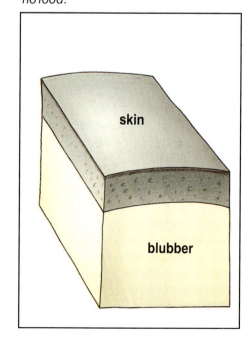

skin

blubber

Staying cool

All animals need to cool down when the weather is hot. Water can help them do this. When water gets hot, it turns into a gas, or **evaporates.** When water warms up and evaporates on an animal's hot skin, the animal's body cools down. Human beings, and some other species of mammal, can produce water from their own skin. This is called **sweating.** Dogs and birds don't sweat, but they pant instead. Water evaporates from their tongue and cools them down. Some animals cool down by covering themselves with water.

Elephants cool off in lakes and rivers by sucking water into their trunk and squirting it into their mouth or over their bodies.

Keeping your foot cool!

You will need:

a pair of clean socks

a bowl of warm water

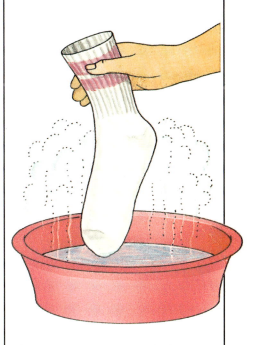

1. Soak one of the socks in the warm water.

2. Put the dry sock on one foot and the wet sock on the other foot.

3. Wait a few minutes. Which foot feels colder? Can you feel the effect of the water evaporating?

Lizards are cold-blooded. Every morning they lie in the sunshine to get warm. The sun's warmth gives these animals energy to move about and hunt for their food.

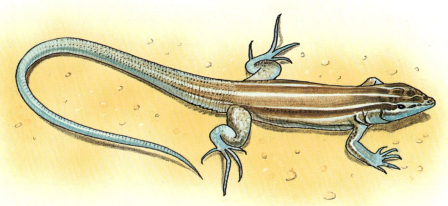

Living in the desert

Would you take an umbrella with you to visit the desert?
It sounds like a silly idea, doesn't it? In fact, it sometimes
rains quite heavily in certain deserts. But the plants and
animals that live there have to be able to survive intense heat
and dryness in between the rains. Sometimes, it doesn't rain
for many months, or even years, at a time.

Small mammals survive the heat by hiding under rocks or stones, or in the sand. They come out only at night, when the air is much cooler.

Some mice and jerboas are so well suited to the dryness of the desert that many don't need to drink water at all. The receive all the water they need in the seeds and plants that they eat, such as cacti.

Bactrian camel

jerboa

Camels are large mammals that can go without food or water for days or weeks at a time! Each camel stores its food as fat in large humps on its back. Its water supply is used up very slowly. But in very hot weather, a large, thirsty camel can drink as much as 53 gallons (200 liters) of water in one day!

horned viper

striped pyxie toad

spiny-tailed lizard

Desert toads spend most of their lives in a deep sleep in burrows underground. When it rains, they come out and lay their eggs in the puddles. The tadpoles hatch and quickly grow into adult toads, which then dig burrows for themselves and wait for the next rains.

A lizard has thick and scaly skin which keeps in moisture. A little water can last for a long time. When the desert becomes too hot for comfort, lizards lie in the shade or under the sand to escape the sun's rays.

The sandgrouse feeds on the seeds of desert plants. It usually flies to drink at a water-hole early each morning. The male sandgrouse carries water back to its young, its soft breast feathers soaked like a sponge with water.

pin-tailed sandgrouse

In order to avoid the heat of the sand, many kinds of lizards lift up one front leg and one back leg at the same time. Early in the day, some lizards might lie on the sand with all four legs off the ground, in order to warm the stomach.

Namib lizard

Desert snakes swallow their prey whole. They can survive because they get all the water they need from their food.

Find out more by looking at
pages **98 – 99**
        100 – 101

Living at the poles

Do you know of a place where it is always cold? There are two places like this, at opposite ends of the earth. The **Arctic** is the area around the North Pole, and the **Antarctic** is the area around the South Pole.

It's so cold around the poles that snow and ice cover both the land and the sea for most of the year. Animals that survive here have different ways of coping with the cold.

female polar bear and cubs

Arctic animals

Polar bears live in the Arctic on islands of floating ice, called **ice floes.** Pregnant polar bears and sometimes female polar bears with yearling cubs spend the cold, dark months on land, in dens they have dug in the snow. They don't actually hibernate because they might freeze to death. Most males and most other females, who do not spend the winter in a den, wander for many miles (kilometers) to find food, mainly seals.

Arctic foxes

The Arctic fox also lives near the North Pole. It has long fur to keep it warm. When snow covers the rocky ground, the fur turns white, but in the warmer months it turns brown or gray. This camouflage means that the fox can sneak up on its prey, small mammals and birds, any time, with little chance of being seen.

It's too cold!

Cold-blooded animals, such as frogs and lizards, cannot live in the very cold polar regions. But some fish can survive, even in seas that are covered by a thick layer of ice. These fish are an important source of food for penguins, seals, and polar bears.

These emperor penguins are huddling together on the ice of the Ross Sea in Antarctica.

This male emperor penguin is about to feed its chick. A milklike substance will go directly from the adult's mouth into the chick's mouth.

Antarctic animals

The female emperor penguin stays at sea during the winter. It never gets as cold there as on land. But the male penguin stays on the land to incubate an egg laid by his mate before she went to sea. The male penguin holds the egg on his feet. He has a thick flap of feathered skin there to keep the egg warm. When the chick hatches, the father bird feeds it a thick, rich liquid, much like the milk of mammals. He produces this liquid in his throat.

When the females return in the spring, all the penguins call loudly, recognizing their mate by their voice. The females then look after the young penguins, and the males go off to sea.

These Indians live and work high up in the Andes Mountains of Peru.

Living on mountains

Have you ever stood on top of a mountain? It is often cold and windy on mountaintops, and there may even be snow. On high mountains, the air is thin. It may contain less oxygen than the amount we need to breathe to stay alive.

You won't find any vertebrates living near the tops of the highest mountains. Even on the lower slopes, it is hard for people and animals to move around on rocky precipices or loose stones. It is even harder to find food.

Mountain people

The Indians of Peru live in a chain of high mountains called the Andes. They breathe air that contains less oxygen than air near sea level. They can do this because their blood contains extra hemoglobin. Hemoglobin is the red substance of the blood. It soaks up oxygen from the air in the lungs. People born at sea level would need an extra supply of oxygen to survive in the same high mountains.

Find out more by looking at pages **86–87**

Mountain animals

All mountain animals have extra hemoglobin in the blood. But their bodies help them to survive in other ways, too. Snow leopards live in the major mountain ranges of central Asia. They have thick coats of fur to retain their body warmth. Their large, furry paws act like snowshoes to keep the leopards from sinking into the snow.

Mountain goats in the Rocky Mountains of North America have hooves with a soft, spongy inner pad surrounded by a hard outer rim. These hooves allow the goat to grip firmly on both rocks and ice, so that it can walk along steep mountainsides.

Flying birds are more at home on mountains than any other vertebrates. But they often have to battle against very strong winds. Usually only the larger birds like eagles nest high up in the mountains. But there is one small bird with strong wings that lives in the Himalaya. This is the Nepalese swift.

mountain goats

bald eagle and chicks

Living in grasslands

Most **grasslands** lie between deserts and humid lands covered with forests. The grasslands began to come into existence about 26 million years ago, when the weather became much drier. Trees do not do well in dry soil. In some parts of the world, such as eastern Africa, the forests began to get smaller. Instead of trees, many smaller plants began to grow. Among them were grasses.

The dry climate encouraged the development of animals which ate small plants. As hundreds of thousands of years passed, the animals became larger and more numerous. These were the ancestors of today's antelopes, zebras, bison, and other grazers. In time, the grazers covered large areas of grassland — the savannas of Africa, the prairies of North America, and the pampas of South America.

Many of these animals, such as the antelope, zebra, and bison, live in large herds. Even though they eat lots of grass every day, the supply of grass never runs out. That's because grass grows from the roots, so even if it is nibbled every day it just keeps growing.

East African grassland

Why is there always grass to eat?

You will need:

three small plant pots

soil or potting compost

grass seeds

seeds of chives or any small flowering plant, such as mustard, mungo, or fennel

scissors

1. Fill the plant pots with the soil or compost. Plant the grass seeds in one pot and the chive seeds in the other two. Water the pots well and add more water every other day.

2. When the plants are 2 inches (5 centimeters) tall, snip off the tops of the potted grass and the chives in one of the pots. Leave the chives in the other pot. In the same way an antelope, zebra, or deer eats the top of the grass when it grazes.

3. Trim the tops of the same plants one week later.

4. Wait another week, then trim the plants in all three pots. How quickly does the grass grow compared with the chives?

African elephant

black rhinoceros

wildebeest

hippopotamus

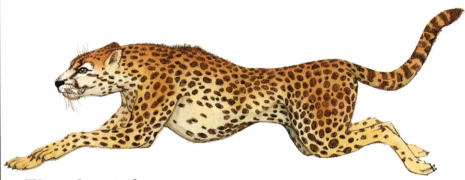

The cheetah

Some of the fastest-moving mammals in the world live in grasslands, where there are large open spaces for running. The fastest carnivore of all is the cheetah. It chases its prey across the grasslands at speeds up to 70 miles (110 kilometers) an hour. Zebras, antelopes and ostriches can run fast, too. They need this speed to escape from their predators.

Living in trees

Can you imagine living on the top floor of a high-rise apartment building and never coming down to the ground? Some animals make their homes high up in the trees of the forest. They find their food there and give birth to their young there. Most of these animals never need to come down to the forest floor.

Large and colorful birds fly around the treetops of the tropical rain forests. A **tropical rain forest** is a forest of tall trees in an area that is warm year-round and has plentiful rain. Parrots, toucans and macaws nest in hollow trees, feeding off nuts, seeds and fruits. In the forests of cooler countries, woodpeckers chip out nest-holes in the trees.

Animals of the forest

Some forest animals travel through the treetops by gliding from branch to branch. Their bodies have special flaps of featherless skin that work like a parachute. Both the flying squirrel and the marsupial glider of Australia have flaps of skin between their front and back legs. The flying draco lizard has flaps of skin on each side of its body. These flaps look like wings. The flying frog has extra-large, webbed feet which act like four tiny parachutes.

The spider monkey's tail is long and muscular. These monkeys can coil their tail around a branch and hang upside down. In this position, they look like spiders!

Sloths are slow-moving vertebrates that walk upside down along the branches. They use their long, hook-like claws to cling on tightly. They can even sleep upside down!

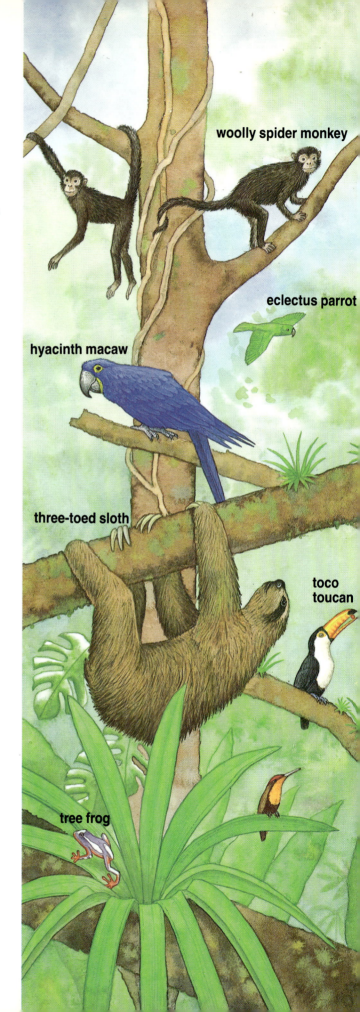

woolly spider monkey

eclectus parrot

hyacinth macaw

three-toed sloth

toco toucan

tree frog

keel-billed toucan

yellow-headed parrot

ruby and topaz hummingbird

tamandua

Frogs in the trees

Tree frogs have tiny, sticky pads on the ends of their fingers and toes that allow them to climb up trees and stick to their branches. They lay their eggs in small pools of water that collect in the hollows of trees, or in plants with saucer-shaped leaves. Some tree frogs carry their eggs and tadpoles with them. They keep them safely tucked in hollows on their back until the tadpoles have grown into young frogs.

This tadpole is lying in a small pool of water that has collected in the hollow of a leaf. As it grows into an adult frog, it will grow two front legs and lose its tail.

A huge variety of animals live in the tropical rain forests of South America.

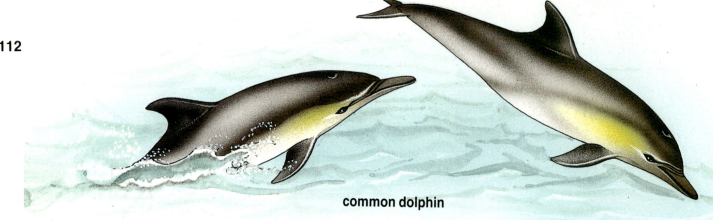

common dolphin

Living in the sea

Most of the vertebrates that live in the sea are fish. Some mammals, reptiles, and birds live there, too. There is only one group of vertebrates not found in salt water. These are the amphibians.

Fish have always lived in the sea, of course. There are more than 13,000 different kinds, or species, living in the sea. But the mammals found in the sea are descended from land animals. They have to come to the surface to breathe, because they have lungs, not gills.

Fish in the sea

Fish come in all sorts of different shapes and sizes. Some are flat so that they can lie on the seabed without being seen. Eels have snakelike bodies. Rays, like the skate, are kite-shaped and seem to fly through the water by flapping their huge "wings."

Mammals in the sea

There are three groups of mammals in the sea—whales and dolphins, seals and sea-lions, and some rare sea mammals called **sirenians,** which include the manatee and the dugong.

There are more than 75 different kinds of whales. The blue whale is the largest animal that has ever lived. It can grow to be as long as 100 feet (30 meters)! Whales need to come up to the surface for air, but sperm whales can hold their breath underwater for over an hour!

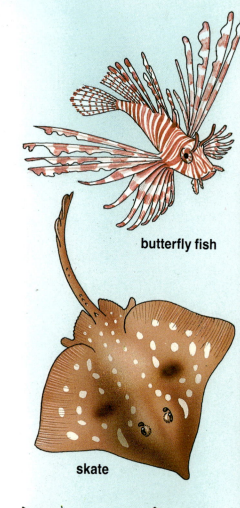

butterfly fish

skate

king penguin

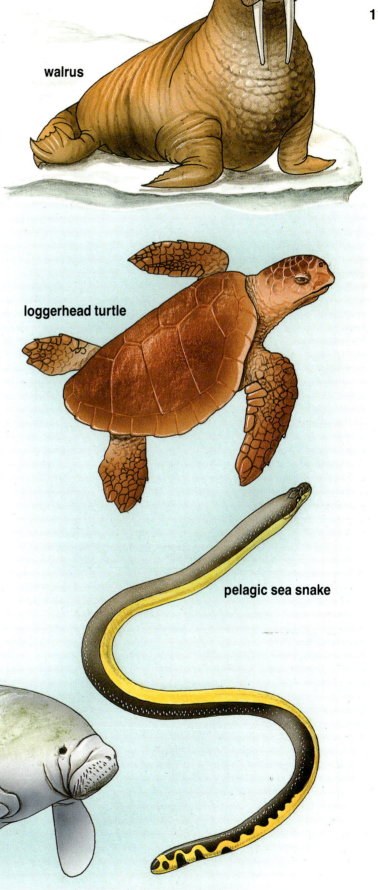

walrus

Dolphins and porpoises are actually small whales. The killer whale is the largest dolphin. Have you ever seen bottle-nosed dolphins perform in an aquarium? They are very intelligent. They communicate with each other by blowing air through their blow-holes to make squeaks, whistles, and clicks.

Seals, sea-lions, and walruses are the only sea mammals that move onto land to give birth to their young. Walruses look like large seals with two long, pointed teeth called **tusks.**

Reptiles in the sea

Some turtles and snakes live in the sea. Like all reptiles, sea turtles are cold-blooded, so they live only in warm waters. The females come out of the sea to lay their eggs in holes on sandy beaches. Most sea snakes never leave the sea. They swim by waving their flattened bodies from side to side and by using their oarlike tails as a paddle.

loggerhead turtle

Birds in the sea

Penguins spend much of their lives in the sea, often hunting fish, their main food. Instead of wings, penguins have flippers which help them to swim. Penguins come to the surface of the water to breathe. They move onto land to lay their eggs and raise their young.

pelagic sea snake

manatee

Living in lakes and rivers

The freshwater lakes and rivers of the world are home to two-fifths of all the species of fish. About 8,400 species of fish live in the lake and river habitats of the world. But many other animals share these waters, too, and are specially adapted to doing so.

Hippopotamuses have short, fat legs and a barrel-shaped body. Although they are one of the largest kinds of mammal, they are very good swimmers.

The water opossum lives in burrows by the water's edge. Its long tail and webbed back legs help it to swim through the water.

The hippopotamus lives in lakes and rivers in Africa. To help it dive for food, it has muscles around its nostrils that can close them completely. The nostrils, eyes, and ears of a hippopotamus are all on the top of its head. It can still see, hear, and breathe, even when most of its body is hidden under the water.

Water opossums are marsupials that live in South America. They carry their young in a pouch, but unlike other marsupials, the water opossum has special muscles it can use to close the top of its pouch. The baby opossums stay safe and dry while their mother dives for food.

Find out more by looking at pages **74–75**

What is a webbed foot?

Have you ever looked closely at a duck's foot? It has a thick flap of skin between each of its three forward-pointing toes. This sort of foot is called a **webbed foot.** Webbed feet act like paddles. They can push back more water, so that a duck can move along faster.

Geese and swans also have webbed feet. So do some mammals that live in water, like the beaver and the duck-billed platypus.

Not all waterbirds have webbed feet. The feet of the jacana are quite different. The jacana's long, thin toes allow it to walk on the leaves of water lilies without sinking into the water.

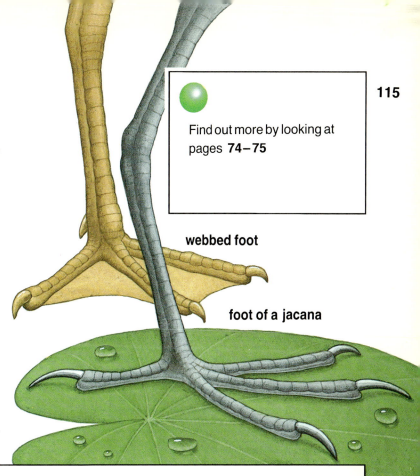

webbed foot

foot of a jacana

The right sort of feet

You will need:

modeling clay

bendable wire

cardboard

scissors

a large baking pan or bowl

water

1. Make model birds of clay with legs and feet of wire. Make the toes on each bird a different length.

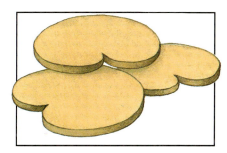

2. Cut out some pieces of cardboard in the shape of lily pads.

3. Put some water in the pan and float the "lily pads." Now try balancing each of your clay birds on a "lily pad." Test each bird with each of the sets of feet.

The longer the toes, the more the bird's weight is spread out. The bird's feet work in the same way as snowshoes or skis, which allow people to move about on deep snow without sinking in.

Which set of feet allows your bird to balance on the "pads" without capsizing them? Can a large bird balance as easily as a small one?

Island animals

Scientists have learned a great deal about how animals survive and grow by studying life on islands. Islands are surrounded by water and cut off from larger areas of land.

Some kinds of animal, such as the kiwi of New Zealand, are found on a single group of islands and nowhere else. Other, very common kinds of animals never reach remote islands at all. And animal species that are found both on islands and on the mainland often live and grow differently in the different areas.

Some animals found on islands are often able to survive because there are no large predators. Sometimes, they even lose their ability to defend themselves! The kiwi can no longer fly, so when human beings brought cats and rats with them to New Zealand, many kiwis were killed.

The Galapagos Islands

The Galapagos Islands lie in the Pacific Ocean, off the coast of South America. Many reptiles, such as lizards and tortoises, live on these islands. They are very different from lizards and tortoises in other parts of the world.

The Galapagos giant tortoise is much bigger than most other tortoises. Lizards called marine iguanas grow to more than 1 yard (1 meter) long. They are the only lizards in the world that swim in the sea and eat seaweed.

kiwi

South America

Galapagos Islands

The marine iguana of the Galapagos Islands is the only kind of lizard that lives in and by the sea. It has a powerful tail to propel its body through water.

The island of Madagascar

Madagascar is an island off the southeast coast of Africa. Monkey-like animals called lemurs have always lived here. They once lived on the African mainland, but they became extinct there. This was because they could not compete with bigger monkeys, which ate the same food and made the same sort of home. If these big monkeys could cross the sea to Madagascar, the lemurs might no longer have enough food or space in which to survive.

Most animals are unable to swim long distances across the sea to islands such as Madagascar. Scientists think that animals reach the islands either by flying, like birds and bats, or by clinging on to a floating mass of logs and weeds. Cold-blooded reptiles have more chance of surviving such a journey than warm-blooded mammals. Reptiles are smaller and don't move about so much, so they need less food.

The monkey-like lemurs live only in Madagascar and the Comoro Islands, off the southeast coast of Africa. They have few enemies because there are few large predators there.

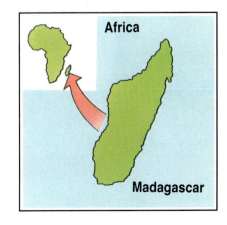

Glossary

Amphibian: Vertebrate that spends part of its life in water and part on land. Amphibians form a *class* (group) of vertebrates.

Arachnid: A type of *arthropod* with eight legs.

Arthropod: Invertebrate whose body is made up of separate sections or segments, with a stiff outer covering, or *exoskeleton*. Arthropods form a *class* (group) of invertebrates.

Bird: Vertebrate with feathers and wings. Birds form a *class* (group) of vertebrates.

Bony fish: Fish with a spine made of hard bone. These animals form a *class* (group) of vertebrates.

Carnivore: Animal that eats other animals.

Cartilage: Tough, rubbery substance, which stretches like elastic.

Cartilaginous fish: Fish with a spine made of *cartilage*. These animals form a *class* (group) of vertebrates.

Coelenterates: *Class* (group) of invertebrates that includes jellyfish and corals.

Cold-blooded: Describes an animal that must move between warm and cold places to maintain a steady body temperature.

Crustacean: Type of arthropod with several pairs of legs.

Echinoderms: *Class* (group) of invertebrates that live in the sea, including starfish, sea urchins, and other animals.

Fossil: Skeleton of a dead animal, or the impression of its body, in very old rock.

Gill: Part of a fish's body that enables it to take in oxygen from the water.

Habitat: An animal's immediate natural surroundings.

Hemoglobin: Substance in blood that carries oxygen from the lungs and around the body.

Herbivore: Animal that eats mainly plants.

Hibernate: To go into an inactive, sleeplike state during a cold period; hibernation lessens an animal's need for food.

Host: Living thing on or in which a *parasite* lives.

Insect: A type of *arthropod* with six legs.

Insectivore: Animal that eats mainly insects.

Invertebrate: Animal that does not have a backbone. Invertebrates form one of the two *phylums* (groups) within the kingdom of animals, and can be divided into six *classes* (smaller groups).

Lungs: In a *vertebrate* living on land, the part of the body where the exchange of oxygen and carbon dioxide takes place.

Mammal: *Vertebrate* whose young develop inside the mother's body until birth and, as babies, feed on the mother's milk. Mammals form a *class* (group) of vertebrates.

Marsupials: Mammals whose young are born in an undeveloped state and then complete development in the mother's pouch.

Metamorphosis: Process of change by an insect from egg to adult insect.

Migrate: To travel a long distance in a large group. The journey is called a *migration*.

Mollusk: *Invertebrate* with a soft body and no bones, which must keep its body moist. Many mollusks have hard shells, inside or outside their bodies. Mollusks form a *class* (group) of invertebrates.

Molt: Break out of an old *exoskeleton* and grow a new, bigger one.

Monotreme: *Mammal* that hatches from an egg instead of being born like other mammals.

Naturalist: Person who watches and learns about living things.

Nutrient: Substance in the soil that helps plants grow.

Omnivore: Animal that eats both plants and animals.

Parasite: Animal that lives in or on other living things.

Pest: Plant or animal that causes harm to other living things.

Placental: *Mammal* whose young are attached to the mother by a cord, or *placenta,* before birth.

Predator: Animal that hunts other animals.

Prey: Any animal hunted, killed, and eaten by another animal.

Reproduction: Process by which living things make copies of themselves.

Reptile: *Vertebrate* with dry skin covered by scales. Reptiles form a *class* (group) of vertebrates.

Scale: Thin, bony plate that covers and protects a fish.

Skeleton: Bony structure inside the body of a *vertebrate,* which includes the spine.

Social insect: Insect that lives with many of its kind in a community where every individual has a role.

Species: Kind of plant or animal.

Spinal cord: Thick bundle of nerves that runs down the back inside the backbone and carries messages from the brain to the rest of the body.

Spine: Long column of bones called *vertebrae* that run all along an animal's back. Also called *backbone.*

Sponge: Underwater *invertebrate* with no head, arms, legs, or internal organs. Sponges form a *class* (group) of invertebrates.

Vertebrae: Bones that make up the spine, or backbone. Some *vertebrates* have vertebrae made of cartilage.

Vertebrate: Animal with a *spinal column* (backbone) and a *cranium* (braincase). Vertebrates form one of the two *phylums* (groups) within the kingdom of animals, and can be divided into six *classes.*

Warm-blooded: Describes an animal that can maintain a steady body temperature.

Worm: Animal with a soft, thin body and no legs. Worms form a *class* (group) of *invertebrates.*

Index

Acknowledgements

The publishers of **World Book's Young Scientist** acknowledge the following photographers, publishers, agencies and corporations for photographs used in this volume.

Cover	Darwin Dale (Science Photo Library); Bruce Coleman, Ltd
10/11	Allan Power (Bruce Coleman Ltd)
12/13	John Taylor (Bruce Coleman Ltd)
14/15	G. I. Bernard (Oxford Scientific Films)
16/17	Michael Chinery
18/19	Michael Chinery; G. Ziesler (Bruce Coleman Ltd)
20/21	Jane Burton (Bruce Coleman Ltd); E. R. Degginger, Zig Leszczynski (Animals Animals)
22/23	Michael Chinery
24/25	Michael Chinery
26/27	Michael Chinery
28/29	J. H. Brackenbury (Bruce Coleman Ltd)
30/31	Michael Chinery
40/41	Michael Chinery
42/43	Jane Burton, Frieder Sauer (Bruce Coleman Ltd)
44/45	C. B. and D. W. Frith (Bruce Coleman Ltd); Michael Chinery
52/53	F. H. Wylie (Frank Lane Picture Agency)
54/55	Jane Burton, Frieder Sauer (Bruce Coleman Ltd)
56/57	ZEFA Picture Library; Allan Power (Bruce Coleman Ltd)
58/59	Michael Chinery; Jane Burton (Bruce Coleman Ltd)
64/65	Jane Burton (Bruce Coleman Ltd)
66/67	Hans Reinhard (Bruce Coleman Ltd)
68/69	John Visser, Rod Williams (Bruce Coleman Ltd)
72/73	Jen and Des Bartlett (Bruce Coleman Ltd)
74/75	J. Cancalosi (Bruce Coleman Ltd)
90/91	Jane Burton (Bruce Coleman Ltd)
92/93	Jane Burton (Bruce Coleman Ltd)
100/101	Jen and Des Bartlett (Bruce Coleman Ltd)
104/105	Francisco Erize (Bruce Coleman Ltd)
106/107	Timothy O'Keefe (Bruce Coleman Ltd)
110/111	H. Rivarola (Bruce Coleman Ltd)
116/117	Gunter Ziesler, O. Langrand (Bruce Coleman Ltd)

Illustrated by

Sue Barclay
Maggie Brand
David Cooke
Marie DeJohn
Sheila Galbraith
Jeremy Gower
Kathie Kelleher
Annabel Milne
Teresa O'Brien
Jeremy Pyke
Gwen Tourret
Pat Tourret

Cover photographs

The fruit fly, or pomace fly, left, is magnified six times larger than its normal size. These flies are a nuisance to fruit farmers.

Lar gibbons, right, live mainly in trees in the forests of Southeast Asia.